ON THE TEACHING OF

Literature

ON THE TEACHING OF Literature

From Charismatic Secrecy to Joyful Revelation

Flemming Olsen

SUSSEX
ACADEMIC
PRESS

Brighton • Chicago • Toronto

2 4 6 8 10 9 7 5 3 1

First published 2016, in Great Britain by
SUSSEX ACADEMIC PRESS
PO Box 139
Eastbourne BN24 9BP

SUSSEX ACADEMIC PRESS
Independent Publishers Group
814 N. Franklin Street, Chicago, IL 60610

and in Canada by
SUSSEX ACADEMIC PRESS (CANADA)

British Library Cataloguing in Publication Data
A CIP catalogue record for this book is available from the British Library.

Library of Congress Cataloguing-in-Publication Data
Applied for.

Typeset & designed by Sussex Academic Press, Brighton & Eastbourne.

Contents

PREFACE

"Is it a worthwhile pursuit to subject the passionate virtuosity of a literary text to closer analysis?" This book answers the question with an unhesitating Yes, and it tackles the natural follow-up question: "How can it be done?"

Literature describes heroism and villainy, betrayal and sacrifice, silent reflection and violent action, love, illness, death, plus, of course, a host of other things. Literature shows us life's possibilities and limitations and the human situation vis-à vis forces that are greater and stronger than man. It initiates us into the greatness as well as the meanness of man. Seeing such powers epitomized in individual characters' struggles, victories and defeats engages a reader's deepest emotions, and it is a remarkable thing that literary experiences can very well be felt to be positive even if they spring from sadness or despair.

There is, then, an intimate relationship between literature and life, and, quite naturally, some scholars have been inspired to look over the shoulders of those who are capable of producing life-like things that are not life. They have found it fascinating to try to understand how authors use the tools of their trade, and they have wanted to communicate their experiences to lights that are, in this respect, lesser than themselves.

The incentive to the writing of this book was twofold: a profound love of literature, and an immense respect for the awe-inspiring task of learning to propagate an awareness of its riches. "Literature" is taken in the sense of fictional texts: newspaper articles, obituaries, hymns, and statistical reports are left out of consideration. A discussion of the problems associated with the communication of literature would seem to be relevant, provided it increases the understanding and enhances the enjoyment of the participants. Perhaps the questions prompted by literary works can be systematized to such an extent that we begin to discern the possibilities of establishing something that may be called literary pedagogy? As a matter of fact, even the institutions that train future teachers have often proved remarkably diffident when it comes to providing their students with some clarification with regard to the core of problems that tend to crop up again and again. In many cases, the teaching has accounted to little more than presentation of various theories and models and leaving the students to draw their own conclusions, pedagogic, aesthetic, or otherwise. A book whose avowed purpose is to be a helpmate to teachers and students alike would seem to be preferable to "implicit pedagogy".

Moreover, within recent years, various branches of science, such as linguistics, psychology and physics have been preoccupied not only with the role of the observer or the analysist, but also with the way in which the observer influences and is, in his turn, influenced by, the object of his analyses. Thus within literary criticism, the Reader Response critics questioned dogmas that had so far been accepted, e.g. about the objectivity of the text, and they conferred an important responsibility on the reader as far as the work with the text, indeed the creation of the text, are concerned. The Deconstructionists went a step further, claiming that a text is really a palimpsest, saying something radically different from what immediately appears. The "actual" meaning of the text is left for the reader to decipher. Similarly, the communication theory has intensified people's preoccupation with the interaction between sender and receiver, and since literature, like language, is a social activity, the teaching of it might conceivably benefit from the findings of the communication theory.

The purpose of this book is to look more closely into some of the problems connected with the teaching of literature, and to suggest and discuss possible solutions. The purpose is also to enable teachers to open their students' eyes and arouse their curiosity. It is commonly recognized that people's understanding and experience of literature is increased and clarified when they compare notes about their reading. This book is intended as a contribution to such exchanges of views. I have tried to avoid two dangers, on the one hand a check-list type of pedagogy with hard and fast inflexible rules, on the other the non-committal chat about "vibes" that the reading of a text may give you.

On the Teaching of Literature is based on the assumption that literature should be seen in terms of a happy combination of art and craft. It does not conform to the principles of any specific or pedagogic ideology. It is pluralistic in that it endeavours to combine various methods and points of view, all the time concentrating on the pedagogic implications of the theories presented. It does not give detailed analyses of individual works. It is not a collection of raised forefingers or a list of prescribed procedures. Throughout the book, the centre of interest is what might be called "intelligent togetherness around texts". References to finicky technicalities are not, in themselves, conducive to the enjoyment of literature; on the other hand, I have no doubt that familiarity with some technical terms and awareness of the mechanisms that a writer makes use of will be beneficial, also for the sake of mutual understanding.

Every text contains a specific as well as a universal element. The specific element gives the work its identity and uniqueness, the universal element makes it point beyond itself – either to other works of art or to what is conventionally called reality. Those two components of a literary work will be the launching pad for many of the questions discussed in the following pages.

The target group is, as the title implies, primarily teachers. However, it is my hope that students as well as amateurs in the original sense of the word, i.e. people who devote some time to literature *con amore*, will find the book serviceable and helpful.

It is a well-known fact that it is neither possible nor desirable to eliminate the subjective ingredient in the treatment of literature. Accordingly, I say unblushingly that is book is mainly what I do and have done, and what I have attempted to achieve, in my career as a teacher. The opinions and evaluations put forward are, basically, some that have been triggered off by my teaching experience. The formulation "experience shows . . . ", which occurs now and then in the book, should be taken to mean "*my* experience has taught me . . . ", but of course it would be absurd to deny that I have been assisted and influenced by the many competent writers whose works are listed in the bibliography, and by successive groups of students whose contributions have sometimes provided illuminating insight. I have studied the Church Fathers with an eye to the communicative usefulness of their assertions. Only, I have often felt the need of adding what might be called a pedagogic dimension to the works of many theorists, for the noble art of teaching has proved to be the playground for quite a lot of high-sounding and well-intentioned commonplaces. To use a terminology that the reader may be familiar with from the field of grammar, I might say that my book is descriptive rather than normative. What it describes is a teacher's practice. The word 'should' that appears fairly frequently expresses my own convictions.

The students referred to are that category of inquisitive and committed readers who want 'to know more'. Since this is not a book about what might be called 'general pedagogy', many practical questions that face any teacher in a classroom (e.g. truancy, disruptiveness, etc.) have been left out of account.

CHAPTER ONE
NON-FICTION VS. FICTION

Non-Fiction

The term non-fiction is used about written texts other than poetry, plays, short stories and novels. Thus it covers e.g. different kinds of journalism, statistical reports, obituaries, and several other categories. If we read a newspaper headline like the following: "American Nobel Prize Winner Optimistic about Chances to Cure Aids", we recognize the item of information as referring to part of what we traditionally call reality: the writer of the article can presuppose some background knowledge in his readers, so he will not have to start from scratch, e.g. by expatiating on what "American" and "Nobel Prize" are. Thus the news item draws on 'outside' sources and is placed firmly in the context of 'our world.' The statement is objectively verifiable. It can be proved or falsified, e.g. by the use of witnesses or searches on the internet. The criteria of truth and falsehood are operative in the sense that the scientist's statement can be assessed or discussed, e.g. with reference to evidence from statistics, biochemistry, and medicine. Some readers may even be able to see whether the scientist – or the journalist quoting his words – withholds decisive material or information, whether he argues his case plausibly and convincingly, etc. Though newspapers may sometimes give slanted versions of a case, it *is* possible to get a precise account of what the scientist actually said. And as readers we may become uncomfortable or annoyed if the content of the article deviates too much from what other sources tell us is the truth.

We can expect the article to inform us, in one way or another, about Aids. It states its subject right from the outset, and we do not take the headline to be an invitation to a game of make-believe. The contents as well as the form of the message are subject to some degree of change; there is scope for variation, one paper may emphasize one aspect that another paper chooses to downplay, but the core of the message remains essentially the same in different papers' versions of it. A newspaper will inform its readers in a more or less intellectual variant of prose: newspaper articles are not normally written in blank verse or as a sequence of sonnets.

It is characteristic of non-fiction texts that they establish some interaction between the text and the surrounding social reality. They *comment on the existing world,* whereas fiction, as we shall see, *creates a new world.* The reader will be wise not to suspend his skepticism when reading non-fiction. Any teacher will know that students tend to be seduced by the seeming objectivity of non-fiction because the subjective element is frequently veiled. For example, a journalist may write, "Everyone agrees that . . . ", or "Only a fool would deny that . . . ", or "Everything goes to show that . . . " instead of the more straightforward (and synonymous) formulation, "I think that . . . " In non-fiction, the narrator is identical with the author. The impression of reliability is reinforced by non-fiction's 'one-level' formulations: a rose is a rose and not a symbol of a beautiful woman. Non-fiction takes its objects, facts and experiences from our world, aiming at maximum perceptibility.

Yet, in a sense, non-fiction has a personal basis: the content of an essay is hardly ever completely depersonalized, and a newspaper article dealing with unemployment is usually more than an enumeration of statistical figures: not infrequently, the journalist's intention is to appeal to the reader's sympathy. Non-fiction may contain some chunks of fiction: long passages of Orwell's *Burmese Days* are really non-fiction fictionalized, i.e. the actual problems surrounding British rule in India are exploited as part and parcel of the plot of the novel; the conversations between Dr Veraswami and Flory are actually dramatized essays.

Reading and understanding non-fiction – an essay, a political speech, an interview, a newspaper article, an obituary notice, etc. – is often an arduous task for students because there is so little small talk in that category of writing. It is a good rule to understand the text and the problem it deals with before starting to discuss it. To ensure his students' understanding of the text, the teacher must use closed questions that follow at the heels of the text, so to speak. The succession of the questions he asks is no less significant since both the information and the chain of argumentation are to be subjected to analysis.

What might be interesting to investigate is, for instance, whether the author informs his readers by patronizing them, by using statistical evidence, by showing his subjectivity, or by ridiculing people who hold a different opinion. Does he account satisfactorily for the premises of his standpoint? Does he withhold or twist information, e.g. when quoting his opponents' views? What use does he make of terms like 'I' and 'because' and their synonyms? Is it a slanted presentation, and, if so, which word or words prove his bias? Does he commit errors of fact? Do we accept his premises? Are his conclusions plausibly and decently derived from his premises, or does he make logical circuits etc.?

In non-fiction, the axioms are relative, it allows little formal variation, its theme is often clearly stated, either implicitly or explicitly, the narrator is identical with the author, and the ending may be an arbitrary pit-stop on life's motorway, as happens in many essays and newspaper articles.

Fiction

"Once upon a time there lived an old king who had three daughters, two of whom were beautiful, the third not so beautiful. One day, the king said to his daughters, 'I intend to invite some princes to find some suitable suitors who will be allowed to marry you . . .'". This mode of presentation prepares a reader for something different from a scientific paper on different traditions of arranging marriages. The reader is invited to step into a world that is not ours, the world of fiction.

"It is not the poet's province," writes Aristotle,[1] "to relate such things as have actually happened, but such as might have happened – such as are possible, according either to probable or necessary consequence." Literature, then, is not only different from reality, but, as Aristotle makes clear in a later passage, "poetry is more philosophical and a more excellent thing than history: for poetry is chiefly concerned about general truth, history about particular".[2]

The writer of a fictional text creates a universe of his own, peopling it with individuals, and providing it with objects. Bourdieu calls attention to the fact that literary criticism has usurped some theological terms to characterize the world of fiction – the creation of an autonomous world and the appeal to imagination *sui generis*.[3] That allows the author to take some linguistic liberties and, more than that, to create worlds that are mysterious, problems that are not explained, and men and women that do not seem to belong to 'our world'.

Though fiction creates its own context, it rarely states its subject as explicitly as does a non-fiction text. When we read, e.g. a novel of several hundred pages, we cannot help getting some idea of what its subject is, but the idea is often based on our power of combination, abstraction, feelings, etc., for in actual fact the subject is rarely stated in so many words. Moreover, fiction does not feel under any obligation to stick to one subject: in novels, digressions are legitimate, part of the novelist's freedom of movement. A fictional text has several possibilities of reference: a rose can denote a plant as well as a beautiful woman – or Christ.

The frame of fiction is created by an author, but presented by a narrator. It may take its starting-point in what we call reality. Thus a good many of the novels of C.P. Snow draw on the conflict between science and the humanities. The opening lines of Jane Austen's *Pride and Prejudice* present and exemplary case: "It is a truth universally acknowledged that a single man in possession of a good fortune must be in want of a wife." That statement belongs to the world of reality: it can be confirmed or denied, and it can be discussed. It sets the scene like a stage direction, and 'the play' can begin a few lines further down: "'My dear Mr. Bennett,'" said his lady to him one day . . . " Entry into the world of fiction is signalled by the shift of the tenses of the verb, from "is" to "said".

The relationship between the two worlds – that of reality and that of fiction – provides a rich field of pedagogic observation. They are not mutually exclusive. The transitions between them are conventionally shown in stories and novels in the tenses of the verbs. Here is Dickens' introduction of Mr. Spenlow in Chapter XXIII of *David Copperfield*: " . . . His gold watch was so massive that a fancy came across me that he ought to have a sinewy golden arm to draw it out with, like those which are put up over the gold-beaters' shops." For a brief moment, the narrator steps out of his universe to make a reference to something in reality with which his readers can be supposed to be familiar. The peculiar status of fiction is illustrated by the fact that a specific term, viz. characters, is used for the men and women who 'perform' in novels, etc. As Professor Bent Nordhjem has pointed out, the characters of non-fiction are immanent in the work; their lives separate from, and independent of, the work are irrelevant.[4] By creating its own universe, fiction sets its own limits. It includes or leaves out things at its own (or rather the author's) discretion. For example, Wordsworth's poem *Lucy Gray* is about a girl who lives with her destitute parents in a lonely rural district. However, we are not told in any great detail about the daily life of the family because that is irrelevant to the point Wordsworth wanted to make. Fiction may even begin at what we consider to be the ending of a story and after that jump back to the beginning. That is what usually happens in detective novels and novels tailored to the same pattern, e.g. Graham Greene's *The Quiet American.*

The purpose of fiction is more than just the recording of facts, for which reason selection comes to be of crucial significance. E.M. Forster achieves a considerable effect in *A Passage to India* by not telling his readers in so many words what actually happens between Adela and Dr. Aziz when they are alone in the Marabar caves. When we read fiction, our knowledge within other fields, e.g. boat building or theology may have to be temporarily, perhaps permanently, put aside.

Fiction does not reveal everything; it is part of its paradigm not to. It is remarkable that though fiction is not primarily intended to give us factual information yet, in the hands of a skillful writer, even the sketchiest outline may deepen our knowledge of ourselves, other people, and the world. Such scenes fascinate students – and may teach them to use, but also to curb, their imagination. For, as a matter of fact, some of the laws that are valid outside fiction also hold good inside it, which means that the basis of fiction is made up of elements that the students will immediately recognize. Yet the information given by fiction differs in kind, not only in degree, from that given by e.g. newspaper articles. More than just recording facts, fiction looks at them from a particular angle and presents them sifted through a temperament. Also, fiction may very well go beyond the world as we know it. That is seen in e.g. fairy tales, science fiction and utopias and dystopias.

Dramas take up an interesting position: the stage directions are located in our universe (think of the detailed stage directions of G.B. Shaw), but the moment the play begins, we are in a different world, which turns out to be a replica of our own. The absurdity of the so-called absurd dramas – another fertile soil for pedagogic analysis – resided in the fact that they were set in a universe that was poles apart from what we live in and have some experience of. They seemed to defy understanding because they did not obey the laws of consistence and logical sequence. And Brecht's theory of 'alienation' (Verfremdung) achieved its effect by its intermittent breaches of the illusion. Why do such breaches happen when they do? What part do they play in the drama as a whole? Can the illusion be preserved? An analogous effect is achieved by 'comic relief', the standard example of which being, of course, the porter's scene in *Macbeth*.

Fiction invites the reader to play a game. Indeed, what Coleridge called 'the willing suspension of disbelief'[5] is indispensable if we are to do justice to and appreciate fiction. "Let's suppose," it says, "that a world exists, inhabited by such and such people, and visited by such and such problems. And what may then happen?" That means that there is considerable similarity between fictional literature and children's games ("Let's pretend that I'm the doctor and you're the nurse"). So, the 'philosophy of as if' is at the root of fiction. The remarkable thing is that neither children nor readers of fiction find any difficulty in separating fact from fiction. When e.g. Malamud says (in the story *The First Seven Years*): "a figure emerged from the snow, and the door opened. At the counter the man withdrew from a wet paper bag a pair of battered shoes for repair", the narrator's intention is obviously not to say: this incident happened ten years ago, or in 1992, but to inform the trader that the text is fiction.

A consequence of the self-sufficiency of fiction is that a fictional work creates its own laws, and they are what the reader has to relate to in a given work. That requires a revaluation of the concept of truth. In 'our' world, truth is a consensus-based (comprehension of) accordance between a given phenomenon and the verbal confirmation, which is universally acknowledged. In the fictional universe, accordance is with one or more of the laws arbitrarily established for a given work and applicable to that work only. Such truth can be neither affirmed nor denied. What happens in fiction must be judged solely by the criteria that are valid in the individual work. Accordingly, it is absurd to censure Shakespeare for making historical blunders, for example in *Julius Caesar*, where Brutus is made to kill Caesar in the Capitol, and not in Pompey' Theatre, which was the actual scene of the murder. In all probability, Shakespeare found it more effective for the theme of his drama to have a tyrant killed in the place where the people's representatives held their meetings. By the same token, we may deplore the fact that Juliet wakes up too late from her induced sleep, and that the delivery of the friar's letter is delayed by the plague, so that Romeo commits suicide because he is under the delusion that his true-love is dead. But 'the given' of Shakespeare's play is that they are not allowed to 'live happily ever after', however meaningless that may seem to us. The axioms of fiction are absolute.

The truth of fiction is the truth of inner coherence and plausibility. A novel may, for example, be psychologically inferior and still be excellent fiction. A character may appear incredible judged by the standards of 'reality', yet he may fall neatly into place in the universe the author has created. The world may never have seen a specimen of the human race comparable to Fagin in *Oliver Twist*, but he is entirely convincing in the set-up of that novel. Animals may speak, persons from outer space may land on Planet Earth, and, like it or not, we are forced to accept it if we want to play the author's game – before we proceed to evaluate his performance. Much of what happens in Pinter's plays seems inexplicable, even meaningless, yet his dramas are not without a particular kind of logic.

The truth of inner coherence is relevant for the teaching as well. The questions that have to be debated where characters and situations in fictions are concerned are, for example, why is that man or woman in the story? Is his or her presence sufficiently accounted for? Is that act convincingly motivated by the story? Is that description compatible with the picture the writer has given us elsewhere in the book of the components of "his" universe?

Assessing the plausibility or inevitability of an incident or a character is not as simple as it sounds, for most readers will be tempted to look upon fiction as if it were fact. Dictators of all ages have always been suspicious of fictional literature – another illustration of the similarity between fact and fiction. However, it is characteristic of works of fiction that no exhaustive or final interpretation of them is possible.

Fiction shows considerable formal variation: different types of verse and prose are the means that the writer uses to 'dress his thoughts'. It is owing to this combination of form and content that fiction is able to give us what is called an aesthetic experience.

The Author

The author is the person who gets the idea for the story, and he decides whether his text is going to be fact or fiction. He arranges the story by subjecting the material he has found to some changes. He determines the setting of the story, the number of characters, the problem to be dealt with and the angle of approach in his treatment. He is responsible for the form of the work and will, in virtually all cases, aim at what he considers maximum perceptibility. He remains hidden, but is an individual who is familiar with our universe, as is seen e.g. when Graham Greene says, "His face was narrow and flat and endless, like an illustration of the law that two parallel lines never meet" (*A Burnt-Out Case*). The author may choose to be a theatre director or a divinity, but he can never disappear.

The Narrator

The narrator is the 'consciousness' that the author chooses as an intermediary between the raw materials of the story and the reader. He is a visible or an invisible agent who is made to report events, describe localities, and quote speakers. He also provides the reader with some necessary background information, e.g. what some of the characters are thinking of. Even seemingly 'neutral recording' ('John sat down') is the result of a narrator's choice.

It is a defining criterion of fiction that it can have, and virtually always does have, a narrator, and it is essential that students familiarize themselves with the distinction between author and narrator. For one thing, a clear understanding of it may anticipate lapses of a biographical kind – think of the many identities that could be attributed to Shakespeare if we were to identify him with his wide range of characters. However, the lyrical 'I', so beloved of the Romantic poets because of their cult of their ego, is a bit tricky (there are few 'I's in Dryden!) because sometimes it *is* actually the author who speaks. In such cases, biographical information is useful.

Secondly, a student who is aware of the distinction will have greater respect for the author's craftsmanship, the skill with which he uses the tools of his trade. An author who is worth his salt will show no little ingenuity in the handling of the narrator's function. Thus, he may obtain really sophisticated effects by letting the narrator be biased, slow-witted, ironical, or even dishonest. Students will love the treasure hunt inspired by such instances.

The Implied Author

The implied author is different from either the author or the narrator. It is the designation used about the sum of values, opinions and attitudes embodied by the book. It may seem slightly unfortunate that such an abstraction should be personified, but that has become a convention within modern criticism. The implied author has no possibility of communication with the reader. Still, in a way he is the author's mouthpiece in that it is thanks to him that some ethical norms and emotional tensions are made manifest in the work so that, after finishing the book, the reader may have a feeling of a complete artistic whole. The implied author's distance to the characters will vary, and, equally, he may be very remote from the reader if the latter does not share or understand the set of values to be found in the book. The 'message' can be conveyed without authorial intervention or narrator's comment, witness the social indignation that permeate many of Dickens' novels. In a teaching situation, it will be a good idea to look at the theme or themes that are found in the text – adding them up may take us closer to the implied author.

CHAPTER TWO

Why Do We Teach Literature

"Studies serve for delight, for ornament, and for ability," said Sir Francis Bacon in his essay *On Studies*. "They perfect nature and are perfected by experience . . . Reading maketh a full man."[1] The very fact that, down through the centuries, men and women have devoted time and energy to the study of literature is strong evidence that literature is a significant factor in the lives of human beings.

Life's existential problems cannot be solved by adding two figures. And if a close friend of yours is dying of cancer, the second law of thermodynamics will be of little assistance to him – or to you. It is true that familiarity with literature will not cure him, but it may perhaps show him that sorrows come to every man, and though his, of course, is felt to be unique, thinking of one or more literary treatments of grief may show him how other men and women in a similar situation have come to grips with it, which may give him some comfort. At least, science is powerless here; it may distract an expert, but it is not a shared experience, and discussing literature is a shared experience. On the other hand, truths that are unassailable from a scientific point of view prove disappointingly unhelpful when it comes to points in our lives that concern us very deeply. That may be one reason why very few fiction writers have taken their inspiration exclusively from the world picture of the sciences. As Meyerhof drily remarks, scientific truths are necessarily valid, but they are not the kind of truths it would be meaningful to risk one's life for.[2]

The great majority of literary works contain, implicitly or explicitly, one or more possible answers to the questions, "How are we to live our lives, how are we to behave to our neighbour, how are we to understand ourselves?" That is, in itself, a weighty argument for devoting one's time to learning about literature and teaching it. We teach literature because its content as well as the thinking it prompts may counteract technology's attempt to reduce man to an automaton and to live his life according to an inflexible timetable. The teaching of literature is based on texts, but inevitably it includes other aspects of life than reading: communication (who says what to whom, why, and with what consequences?), psychology (why does that character react as he does in the situation?), perhaps some history (to what extent are the events described in the book in accordance with historical facts?). On top of it all is aesthetics (the delight we take in form, and the respect we feel for the artist's struggle with his chosen medium).

Some people might be inclined to object that the teaching of literature only serves to perpetuate an antiquated cultural and elitist ideal, and to support the conception that dusty institutions should by their very existence be revered. Other people might be afraid that literature would lose its charm, perhaps even its characteristics and peculiarity, if it is placed on a Procrustes' bed of classroom exercises.

However, everything depends on the way literature is taught. There is, incontestably, an element of manipulation in all teaching. But it should not be forgotten that students expect, and therefore are not averse to, some degree of manipulation. Besides, teachers cannot hold a candle to advertising experts as far as manipulation is concerned. Only, the latter are applauded for it and make big money on it.

Teaching literature is not tantamount to inculcating a set of conventions for what is, and what is not, good literature, in a group of recipients. Nor is it a matter of forcing some opinions and clichés down defenceless students' throats. And the object is certainly not to prove that a reader ought to be ashamed of feeling intuitive or emotional ('superficial') pleasure when reading a book. Literary pedagogy is not least a question of someone who knows more joining hands with someone who knows less and wants to know more, between them using their common sense. Together, they are on a game-shooting 'spree' – sometimes they succeed, and sometimes they fail. Most of the skills that students need in order to carry out their jobs in later life can be learnt at appropriate institutions. But it is not until they meet literature that they are given a real chance to understand what it can mean to live.

In modern theories of language acquisition, a distinction is made between two aspects of language, viz. the *instrumental* one and the *integrative* one. Instrumentality comprises everything that is immediately useful to the language user in his daily life, e.g. in situations where he is to ask, inform, advise, etc. another person. Instrumentality, as the name implies, looks upon language in terms of a tool, and the movement of it can be described as *centrifugal*, i.e. *from* the individual *towards* the world surrounding him. 'Integrativeness', on the other hand, contributes to shaping the personality of the individual and to enriching his potentialities. Thus, the movement is *centripetal*, the emphasis being on the powerful impact that learning and using his mother tongue or a foreign language may have on a human being, rather than with what he can do with it once he has mastered it.

Like all art, literature serves integrative purposes. The remarkable thing is, however, that 'integrativeness' goes hand in hand with what may be called a derived instrumentality. At first sight, some of the universes that we meet in literature may seem unfamiliar or even repellent. But we soon discover that literature shows us a gamut of possibilities of tackling the problems of life. We will become familiarized with ways of thinking and acting that differ from our own, and our eyes will be opened to the fact that, everywhere and in all ages, life has been anything but simple.

Also, literature combines a public aspect and a private one: it is public in that it is not the prerogative of an exclusive elite, for of course everyone is free to borrow or buy books. It is private because my understanding and experience of a work of art need not coincide with anyone else's However, experience shows that the relevance and value of literature actually seems to increase when public meets private: when a group of people discuss a literary work, each group member tends to feel that the text becomes greater, richer, and more profound (perhaps also more challenging and incomprehensible!) than at the time when it was 'only' private. That means that literature is good teaching material and that recipients benefit from the community of learning.

According to Horace's *Ars poetica,* the influences of literature on its readers were to be those of *prodesse et delectare,* i.e.to instruct and to delight. The instruction, or benefit, that literature can give to its readers – and to which teaching may open students' eyes – is of several types. It may for instance be historical, sociological, or psychological documentation and illustration: some literary works give just as much and just as precise information as newspaper articles. If a person wants to know how demagogy can influence an impressionable mob, he can do no better that read Mark Anthony's funeral speech to Caesar in Shakespeare's *Julius Caesar.* By the same token, *Othello* will give a reader a vivid impression of what jealousy *is,* more richly facetted than an article in a scientific paper. Literature is at the same time 'outside' our universe in that it creates a world of its own and 'inside' our life in that its world has numerous points of similarity with ours. One difference is that literature can take over where statistics and the social sciences stop.

The teaching of literature should also aim at arousing and stimulating the curiosity and fascination of the students, for the second leaf of Horace's diptych has parity of esteem with the first. Writers of all ages have expressed views on the existential problems that have always posed themselves to all human beings. A teacher will have no difficulty in pointing out how authors from Homer down to our own age have dealt with the problems of the individual in his relation to himself, his neighbor, the world around him, and his creator. And, with all due respect to technology, those issues are not likely to be outdated. The content of literature pleases, not only in the sense that it may give the reader (or spectator) a good laugh. More than that, in its very essence literature contains a challenge that tempts man's exploring spirit, and the accompanying state of mind is composed of pleasure and excitement, and in some cases relief. Literature works with a combination of what the reader knows and what he does not know: there is a problem – here are one or more suggested solutions.

The content of literature is often awe-inspiring and terrifying, to the experienced reader as well as to the beginner, in that it teaches us that we stand on the shoulders of centuries of predecessors. As *Ecclesiastes* has it, 'there is no new thing under the sun'.[3] But the form of literature also gives pleasure: to analyse and pursue the thought embodied by literary works and to pay attention to the author's painstaking and often provocative use of language can be a source of inspiration, provided that the teacher has been capable of opening his students' eyes to the wondrous world. As in the visual arts and music, the form of literature is inseparable from the content, but it is not always felt to be as immediately 'given' as in the other arts. Accordingly, the students' attention has to be directed towards formal aspects, but once formal awareness is acquired, even fairly young students can find aesthetic satisfaction in working with a poem that is also formally successful.

The linguistic aspect of literature is interesting for several reasons. Coleridge called words "living powers by which things of most importance to mankind are activated, combined, and humanized".[4] Especially in the masterpieces of literature, we witness the fortunate interaction of the living language and the creativity of a genius. We sense how, through his selection and planning, the author has endeavoured to defeat the diffuseness and triteness of much everyday communication. At its best, the teaching of literature will not only sharpen the students' awareness of the potentialities of language, but also encourage experimentation and creativity on the part of the students. And he who knows many words has a more *nuancé* view of life than he who knows only a few.

'Learning' literature enables the students to form opinions, make decisions and give reasons for their standpoint. But, over and above that, in the 'classroom' situation, students will learn to be at the receiving as well as the giving end, and the exchange of ideas and suggestions, the fertile 'cross-fertilization' that is the outcome of successful teaching will train the students' talent of presentation, argumentation, analysis, and evaluation. And it should be added that the person who is at the centre is not permanently and necessarily the teacher.

The object of teaching literature should not be to try to pinpoint what literature is, but rather to show how it has been used, in all ages, by those who practise it. Nor should the purpose be to provide students with one or more self-styled exhaustive theories, but rather to make them familiar with some of the tools that can profitably be used, and some of the questions that can reasonably be raised in dealing with texts. Once you have determined what an author says and how he says it, you have taken a step on the road to literary understanding and literary experience.

What would happen to civilization if, during their years of education, pupils and students were given only narrowly technical books to study? Or supposing that the texts used in foreign language teaching were nothing but mechanical drills? What would happen to a society that was forced to find its spiritual nourishment in inane advertising slogans and journalistic commonplaces? The perspective is frightening, for the mental health of such a society would be jeopardized. Not everybody regards – or can be made to regard – literature as a revelation, and not everybody is capable of feeling a thrill of pleasure when coming across a felicitous formulation. But experience shows that the great majority of students have an innate sense of language that is well worth cultivating. Also, that precision and variation in linguistic habits can be trained. Couldn't it be said that it is any society's duty to see that its citizens are not intellectually under-stimulated, not to say starved? Literature is not a harmless game of make-believe. Rather it can be regarded as a ‘seventh sense’, enabling us to see what our eyes do not see, and to hear what our ears do not hear.

CHAPTER THREE

LITERATURE AS TEACHING MATERIAL

Literature unfolds worlds to us and depicts a multiplicity of human beings. Since it also conveys ideas, our dealings with literature inevitably cause us to question some of our opinions and convictions. The fact that it is art does not imply that it is the opposite of life. Rather, it is an intensification of life, a 'heightening', as the Neo-Classicists would call it, that cannot help influencing the minds of its readers. That is, in itself, a weighty argument for devoting some time and energy to literature, for learning about it and for teaching it.

The ideals of classical physics and mathematics were quantifiability, causality and determinism. Those attributes, if correctly used, were held to be capable of giving us a reliable picture of reality, and they came to be recognized as standards for other branches of human knowledge. That explains why literary criticism was for many years on the defensive: its results could not live up to what was considered a basic scientific requirement, viz. an amount of objectivity on a par with that which was supposed to apply within the sciences.

The outcome was not only that 'genuine' science tended to turn up its nose at the methods and achievements of literary criticism, but also that literary criticism itself strove to reach a goal that was to all intents and purposes incompatible with the essence of literature. The popularity of stylistics was probably due to its seeming susceptibility of 'scientific' treatment by means of frequency analyses and statistics. But generally, the benefit a reader might derive from a work – be it emotional engagement or increased insight – was liable to be looked askance at because it could be neither measured nor counted.

One of the most interesting developments within the scientific thinking of the last decades is that subject and object may not be as sharply separated as Descartes taught people to believe they were. It is no longer tenable to talk about objective descriptions in the sense that they are uninfluenced by the scientist's test set-up. To put it differently, one might say that a scientist's findings are to some extent predetermined by the way his experiments are carried out, thus becoming self-fulfilling prophecies. To some extent he will find what he is looking for. What this boils down to is, first, that the dividing line between the world 'out there' and the mind 'in here' is being blurred; secondly, that we no longer have one reality, but different ways of describing it. Indeed, there are differing, but equally correct, descriptions of some part of reality, depending on the point of view that is adopted. The 'absurd' dramatists represented that view. The subjective element of science is also borne out by numerous statements from outstanding scientists to the effect that it was their preoccupation with art – e.g. the study of literature or music – that nourished their curiosity and fertilized their imagination.

A parallel can be found within linguistics, which increasingly concentrates on the relationship between language and reality. Some anthropologists opine that 'reality' is an entity that is more or less constructed by the categories of the human language, and they have proved that different cultures live in different worlds.

To a given group, "'the real world' is to a large extent unconsciously built up on the language habits of the group," said Edward Sapir as far back as in 1929.[1] The so-called Imagists, writing in the first two decades of the 20th century, objected to the scientific view of reality, claiming that the truth revealed in a poetic image (hence the name given to the writers) was as reliable and convincing as a description based on exact scientific data.[2]

The two views – that of science and that of art – cannot be kept in watertight compartments, but one important difference was pointed out by Northrop Frye: science develops, i.e. today we know more about that which we call the world than did Newton and his contemporaries. But literature is not characterized by a similar progression: there is no rising curve of e.g. imaginative richness, and the fact that a dramatist is posterior to Shakespeare is no guarantee that his drama will be better that *King Lear*.[3]

But though – or perhaps because – literature is timeless, it can make us familiar with some of the great movements of the European cultural tradition, thus putting our own age in an appropriate perspective. Thus, the 20th century's idea of man was largely anticipated by the Renaissance, and numerous examples of 'the spirit of our age' are reminiscent of some that we find in 19th century Romanticism, e.g. the attitude to children and to what was called 'the noble savage', the abuse of drugs, the nationalist movements, utopias and the cult of unspoiled nature. Such knowledge is given added significance when the political and social repression that set in after Romanticism is remembered.

It is a well-known fact that literary works give pleasure on several levels. Thus many fairy tales contain a story that has an immediate appeal to children and simple minds. However, more experienced readers will have no difficulty in 'digging beneath the surface' and finding a moral, or even a philosophy of life, in such texts. Allegory is an analogous case; an allegory is a story which is also a story about something else, e.g. a symbol of an underlying idea. Finding a symbol or a moral in an allegory is an appreciated treasure hunt to most students. Hopefully, working with such texts will sharpen their attention to the equivocal nature of many political statements. Some politicians have acquired considerable virtuosity in seemingly speaking about one thing, but in actual fact referring to something quite different. It is a well-known fact that some writers of fiction have proved to be acute and visionary social thinkers and analysts, and have revealed intuitive insights into the workings of the human mind comparable to those of a professional psychologist.

Literature is not superior to 'real life' in the sense that it is more important to be able to judge a character in a play that to size up a fellow who wants to sell you a second-hand car. And there is little evidence to show that reading good literature necessarily raises a reader's moral standards or deters him from doing evil. Whereas science pretends that it takes 'the world we live in' as its starting-point, art, including literature, admits that it creates a world, which it proceeds to attempt to make convincing. Admittedly, its solutions are often indefinite and tentative, but literature can help put its readers on their guard against facile or over-simplified solutions. A newspaper article describing a catastrophe is not likely to give its readers any enjoyment, but the remarkable thing is that the same scene in a novel may send a thrill of æsthetic pleasure down the reader's spine – maybe because he knows that it is 'mere fiction.'

The German philosopher Schopenhauer is quoted as saying that reading means thinking with somebody else's head than your own. Something happens to a person when he becomes a reader – perhaps he finds a brother or a fellow-sufferer in the text. Basically, literature provides its readers with a far more richly faceted picture of life than that given by science.

In the great majority of cases, a math teacher will find it possible to have a mental list of acceptable solutions to the problems he puts to his students. Not so his colleague, the teacher of literature: of course he can reject errors of fact out of hand ('Shakespeare died in 1848') as well as postulates based on evident misunderstandings of the text. But the teacher of literature is often given answers that, even if they are obviously not perfectly correct, yet cannot be rejected categorically, for they may be capable of taking us one step further. Objections like 'However, on the other hand . . . ', or 'Yet, a few lines further down . . . ' are rarely heard in a math class. As was mentioned above, it is of crucial importance that, to all parties involved, a literature class becomes synonymous with togetherness – perhaps even intelligent togetherness – with the day's text at the centre.

Teaching literature is not like teaching any other subject, for on top of all the points mentioned above, there is the ethical aspect. The teaching of literature potentially influences the recipients profoundly, and the experiences it gives the individual may radically alter the standards he or she brought with them to the class. Accordingly, a teacher should use no little tact and caution in the pressure he brings to bear on his students in order to prompt reactions on their part. Literature is not a mechanical string of words, and understanding literature is different from understanding a cause and effect sequence in history. So the teacher should be aware that he is likely to engender complicated, sometimes violent, reactions in his students. And he cannot take the easiest way by saying 'Your guess is as good as mine', which, if too often repeated, will be taken as a sign of incompetence by the recipients: they have come to the class to be decently informed.

CHAPTER FOUR
THE TEXT

The Latin word *textum* means 'tissue' (from the verb *texo*, I weave), and, by extension, 'the cohesion of speech'. Quintilian uses it in the sense of 'the style of a literary work'.[1] *The Longman Dictionary of Contemporary English* lists the following definitions: (1) any written material; (2) the writing that forms the main part of a book, magazine, etc., rather than the picture or notes; (3) a book or other piece of writing that is connected with learning or intended for study.

For literary criticism, definition 3 is relevant: a text is a series of linguistic symbols from which it is possible to derive meaning. What is interesting is that, on closer analysis, the concept of text will be seen to have several characteristics in common with those of a game (as Wittgenstein pointed out), viz. rules, limitation, order, combination, and selection. A number of significant modern theories and models have not questioned those basic principles, but they have stressed different aspects of the game. They are all concerned not so much with what a text is, but rather what it is capable of doing, meant to do, or made to do.

The *communication model* conceives of the text as a message: both a sender and a receiver are required, and of course either of the parties has some opinions, attitudes and values, etc. But in order for communication to be at all possible, the two parties must have some ideas of what communication is, or can be, i.e. they have to agree on some rules, e.g. as to how the sender can encode his message into the text, and how the receiver can subsequently decode it. The model has interested linguists because it includes stylistic factors ('how?') as well as emotional ones ('with what result?').

Already Francis Bacon was, perhaps unwittingly, aware of some of the pedagogic potentialities of the communication model; if misunderstanding arises, "the error is both in the deliverer and the receiver. He that delivereth knowledge desireth to deliver it in such a form as may be soonest believed and not as may be easiest examined."[2]

Bacon's words cover not only propaganda, they also say a good deal about the way many a non-fiction writer will sugar the pill to facilitate the acceptance of his message.

However, it can be doubted whether it is wise to adopt the communication model uncritically and as the only instrument of literary analysis. For one thing, the receiver of a literary work is of dubious identity, and sender and receiver are remote from each other, in terms of time as well as of space. Ordinary linguistic utterances have what may be called a situational context, but a literary work is under an obligation to create its own context. In a normal communication situation, both sender and receiver are able to're-establish' a message if it is somehow jammed. In literary communication, the interpreter will often have to choose the interpretation that, in his opinion, seems to tally with the truths that he has found operative in the universe created by the sender. He cannot *ask* the sender. Add to this, the literary message is fiction, i.e. the referential function of the linguistic utterance has been altered.

Still, as a pedagogical instrument, the model has some advantages, especially in the case of beginners, being applicable to all types of text, and having no ideological or theory-laden strings attached. An added advantage is that, with its simple terminology, it is serviceable as an opening gambit also to beginners among students.

The *biographical model*, which was ultimately initiated by the 19th century French critic Sainte-Beuve, attempts to prove some interdependence between the author's life and background and his works. Few people would deny that a causal relationship can be demonstrated between Hemingway's own interests and beliefs and the plot of his novels and stories. By the same token, critics have been at pains to detect an element of personal suffering in Shakespeare's sonnets. Of course an author's works do not exist in a vacuum, but the relationship between his biography in the widest sense of the word and his oeuvre is more than a case of simple stimulus–response causality. The technique is very popular, especially among beginners, who devote a considerable amount of energy to finding 'obvious' parallels, but who tend to overlook the fact that the model excludes the *persona* of the narrator. That means that the artistic processing of possible biographical material is ignored, and the work of art is overshadowed by extra-textual information.

The *structuralists* look upon the text as a finite system of signs within the greater system of language: the individual artist's achievements are manifestations of the greater system called language. Saussure's *langue/ parole* dichotomy is not far away, and the model has been applied within other fields of experience than linguistics, e.g. anthropology, sociology, and psychology. Before a text can be explained, the structuralists say, its structures must be described. The significance of the individual items depends on their place and function in the structures.[3] Learning to understand a text means becoming able to grasp some of the ways in which the parts of a complex system are connected. I.A. Richards pointed out that such a process of understanding is quite analogous to what happens in the process of reading.[4] As every teacher knows, it is by no means an easy task to find out what the text says, and what it does not say, and the structuralist approach trains readers to follow the development of the text and to discipline their imagination when working with the text.

The advantage of the model as a teacher's tool is that it teaches the students to read a text carefully. At first sight, it might seem a good idea to examine the building bricks of the larger components of a 19th century novel, e.g. the functional significance of the 'inset stories' that appear in many of Dickens' novels. The drawback is that it is difficult to 'teach' structures, partly because they tend to become unwieldy and inaccurately defined, partly because it is uphill work to account for what one actually understands when 'understanding' structure. And it has proved a serious bone of contention to decide which of the structures in a text are relevant, and which are not.[5]

Furthermore, there is a risk of it degenerating into inane hair-splitting with complete disregard for the overall synthesis of the text. The German derogatory term *Kleinphilologie*, i.e. excessive concentration on minutiae at the expense of a larger whole, comes to mind here. Also, its doctrine that a text should be regarded as an isolated entity, free of any extraneous context (New Criticism's argument) has proved untenable. In the cases of shorter poems, many of which are sophisticated jigsaw puzzles, the model will often surpass any other approach, but it is of limited usefulness where larger contexts, e.g. novels, are concerned.

It will be seen that the communication model and the biographical model are 'man-orientated', whereas structuralism is 'text-orientated', indeed it depersonalizes literature. To the structuralists, aesthetic satisfaction consists in showing connections, parallels, contrasts, etc. in the text, and in demonstrating how the interaction of parts and wholes is of paramount importance for the understanding and enjoyment of the text.

The *Marxists* have other (and bigger) fish to fry: they want to prove that all significant literary works express the world view of a particular social class. To them, the interest of a text resides in what it enunciates about a given society.

No doubt, several 19th century novels are all the better explained after being put in the mould of a competent Marxist reading, witness e.g. Lukacs' and Goldmann's penetrating studies on the correlation between the concept of 'bourgeoisie' and the 19th century novel, whereas Romantic poems have proved less cooperative. The obvious weakness of the model as a pedagogical instrument is not only its rigidity, which forces it to exclude 'deviant' suggestions, but also the fact that the outcome is a foregone conclusion: the analyst knows what to look for, and of course he finds it. The consequence is that the exhilarating experience of sailing into uncharted waters loses a good deal of its attraction. And if a reader's main purpose is to gather information about social relations, would it not be preferable to read some social or economic history? Sometimes it may seem as if Marxists are fascinated by other features than aesthetic ones. Thus they show little or no interest in the kind of insight into universal experiences that e.g. psychological criticism has given us. Finally, the Marxists' criteria for quality come to differ from those of non-Marxists because, to the former, both popular and more substantial types of literature are interpreted as symptoms of false consciousness.

Reader Response criticism somehow makes the reader a 'co-creator' of the text. Its postulate is that the category of literature is largely established by a consensus among a group of readers. They also maintain that there is always a text, but what is 'in' it is subject to variation.[6] The dispute about the nature of the text has some awe-inspiring implications: what is ultimately at stake is the question of the existence of the world. If a text is proved to be a social construct, what about the world? The Reader Response critics hesitate to assert that man creates the world, and their terminology admits words pointing to a difference between 'I' and 'the world'. It seems that they are bolder in their ideology than in the concomitant epistemological inferences.

The number of orthodox Reader Response adherents is dwindling, which is perfectly understandable. They say that the reader's creative participation is constitutive of the text. According to Stanley Fish, interpreters do not decode poems: rather, they create them by a series of operations that are circumscribed by the patterns of understanding that are valid in a given age.[7] Every age has some 'interpretative paradigms' beyond which criticism cannot move. Thus it is ensured that literary texts are provided with recognizable forms.

The theory is not only empirically dubious – thus, Fish et al. do not specify what kind of people qualify to be members of the deciding groups – it is also pedagogically hopeless: if the reader creates the text, how do we decide which of the readers has the better explanation? And where does the author come in? Are the dactyls of the opening lines of Tennyson's *The Charge of the Light Brigade* something the readers 'read into' the text? The rhythm is meant to imitate the sound of galloping horses, and it is objectively given in the text. The opening chapters of Fielding's novel *Joseph Andrews* are intended as a parody of Richardson's

Pamela. A reader can establish alternative legitimate readings of Fielding's novel – the reader may e.g. concentrate on the social picture that emerges in the novel – but the satirical element, placed there by the author, has to be included in any honest interpretation of the novel.

There are numerous examples where the subject circumscribes or influences the reader's creative potential. Elegies cold be mentioned as examples. Authors' autobiographies prove that the author does not just jot down any number of words, and a text cannot mean anything under the sun. That does not mean that the reader's role is utterly negligible. The reading process is not passive consumption, but active digestion of what the author offers. Goethe put it like this:

> Leser, wie gefall' ich dir
> Leser, wie gefállst du mir?[8]

The text has objective existence before meeting the reader in so far as it contains potentialities of triggering off responses in the reader.

The *impressionistic model* makes the reader's spontaneous reactions the touchstone of his meeting with the text. There is some impressionism in all teaching of literature since every teacher will do his best to urge his students to practise an empathetic, i.e. more that reason-based, reading of the text. And the model is not without pedagogic advantages in that most students do not mind communicating and discussing the impression made on them by a text – actually that is the point where much textual work starts. Yet the ground is slippery. As the name indicates, the ultimate basis is a personal impression, which means that the model is even less empirically based than the others mentioned in this chapter. In the hands of an expert reader, the model may provide valuable insight, indeed glimpses of sublimity. However, the great majority of students have neither the experience nor the intuition that are required for such soaring flights. And there is the additional risk that the use of the model may obstruct the progress of any deeper analysis. It may sacrifice the text for the sake of the 'felt' response evoked by it.

The *Deconstructionists* claim that there is no single explanation of a piece of writing. They are careful readers like the New Critics, but they go several steps further in their pretence that a text is actually a palimpsest behind which one or more alternative senses are hidden. The procedures they follow to find the hidden meanings are obscure, and that is what makes the model unusable in a teaching situation – the model is pedagogically speaking a blind alley, unfit for students' consumption. At best, it would only serve to confuse them, at worst to irritate them, because everything seems to be connected to everything else, and there are no limits to what words can mean or refer to.

Some 20th century language theorists like Charles Sanders Peirce, John Searle and John Austin have dug a little deeper into the communication model and have analysed what they call speech acts.[9] Evidently, a sentence is not just a succession of sounds: it has a semantic content that is obvious to the users of the language of the sentence. What the speech act theorists have shown is that, over and above the semantic content, every statement also indicates something about the *way* in which it is to be understood.[10.] Thus the sentence 'I'm coming on Friday' can be an assertion, a promise, a threat, etc. The context and the speaker's tone of voice decide which of the overtones is to be valid. The point is that content is more than semantics: no statement is ever 'pure' without reference to a context. The speech act theorists claim that the semantic part of a statement is embedded in what they call its 'illocutionary force', i.e. its 'innate' indication of the way the sender intends it to be understood.

The relevance of this theory for texts is obvious. A text never exists in a vacuum, but is related to a context. Since a text contains more than a series of dictionary definitions, it is understandable that it can be taken to mean different things by different readers. If one thinks for a moment of the complications surrounding the drawing up of laws and legal documents, one will immediately realize the justification of the statement that 'much depends on the way you interpret it'.

Non-fiction texts often have a strongly perceptible illocutionary force: buy this product, believe this statement, and distance yourself from this ideology. However, fictional text, too, have some amount of illocutionary force, albeit in a more indirect way: enjoy me, it say, it says; or, feel entertained; or, admire my formal perfection. What is called the moral of a text becomes part and parcel of its illocutionary force: sympathize with this character, criticize this behavior, etc. That is probably the justification for the frequently heard opinions about what a text 'wants to say'.

Most schools of criticism have taken the text to be a unique and identifiable entity, something that has an objective existence of its own. In that case, criticism becomes the study of the correct manner or manners of tackling a text. There is an ancient tradition in Western thinking that Truth is One. But, concurrently, it has been acknowledged that the profound and significant pronouncements of literary works are susceptible of a rich crop of interpretation.

However, in cases where two or more competent critics have different, perhaps conflicting, views on the meaning of a text, it is no easy matter to decide which of them is right. Usually, disagreement is over more than the exact meaning of one or two words in the text. Critics' conflicting interpretations will sometimes lead to the existence of totally different texts, which happens, for instance, if one critic takes the text at face value, whereas the other understands it as being ironical. To pursue the analogy between a text and a game that was suggested in the opening paragraphs of this chapter, one might say that the critics in question have different rules for their play. This is where the Reader Response critics' idea of a brotherhood of competent readers may acquire some relevance: some readings will, by general consensus, be more plausible than others, which is not tantamount to saying that 'deviant' readings are always to be avoided.

My own working definition of a text as far as the teaching of literature is concerned is the following: 'a man-made document, existing in a reproducible form and susceptible of being made pedagogically serviceable'. The document may be a book, a newspaper article, a film, a graphic novel, a TV programme, a tape recording or a digitalized piece of writing. The document may describe, discuss, criticize, judge, evaluate, comment on, or discourse on, fact or fiction. The peculiarity of the text is that it is at the same time unique and attached to a specific context, i.e. it is dependent on some factors in space and time outside itself. But the text in the sense of written signs on a page or a computer screen exists prior to any interpretation.

The reproducibility of the text is a consequence of its status as a document: it must be feasible to perform, show, or read the same passage or passages over and over again, return to them, etc., with the assurance that the signs do not change, but perhaps the meaning read into them. Modern criticism has expanded the concept of text so as to cover also what happens e.g. in a classroom in a teaching situation. But unless it is somehow recorded, it is not possible to return to such a situation and find it identical with its first occurrence. Accordingly, such cases fall outside the limits of my definition.

Some Criteria of Appropriateness

In theory, all texts contain a core of teaching potential. Experience shows, however, that some texts are more 'teachable' than others. The immediate answer to the question of what texts we should teach would be valuable texts. But things are not as simple as that, for value in literature turns out to be just as elusive as the concept of literature itself. Furthermore not every valuable text is *eo ipso* suitable teaching material.

Different ages have had different literary ideals. The Neo-Classicists strove to discipline their formulations so as to make them coincide with the standard poetic diction of that age. Imitation was one of the conditions to be met if the text were to qualify as 'good'. The Romanticists preferred texts that were evidence of "the spontaneous overflow of powerful feelings", as Wordsworth put it in the Preface to *Lyrical Ballads*. Even Shakespeare is subject to changes of taste. Matthew Arnold said about him "Others abide our judgment; thou are free", but 18th century dramatists like Dryden and Nahum Tate had made adaptations of his plays. The New Critics gave a new lease of life to 17th century metaphysical poets like Donne.

The critical commonplace *'de gustibus non disputandum'* means that it is impossible to write a thesis (disputare) on criticism as such because tastes vary with the ages (gustibus is the plural). It is sometimes wrongly interpreted to mean that it is impossible to discuss the criteria that an individual or an age exalts in to principles or dogmas. That interpretation is untenable, for such discussions are the staples of what we call literary criticism.

The idea of quality may be pushed further. Thus, on a superficial view, it might seem plausible to say that violence and brutality are incompatible with quality. Yet nobody would deny that *King Lear* has value even if Gloucester has his eyes put out on the stage. Horace's advice to the dramatist, "Let not Medea slay her children before the audience" was probably deduced from Greek tragedies, in which the catastrophe usually takes place off stage and is reported by a messenger – as happens in *Macbeth,* when the protagonist kills old King Duncan. Horace's advice is a useful rule of thumb, and most people would agree that unrelieved wallowing in violence rarely, if ever, makes for quality. On the other hand we know that disgusting or even pornographic details can be successfully integrated in the artistic unity of a literary work – because they are details. The upheaval originally caused by D. H. Lawrence's *Lady Chatterley's Lover* seems to have subsided, and Henry Miller's *Quiet Days in Clichy* has acquired cult status. And sophisticated turning of the screw – as in Albee's *The Zoo Story* – certainly leaves its effect on the reader or spectator. Besides, if we expect literature to confirm the idea of a just world in which the good are rewarded and the wicked duly punished (characteristically that kind of justice is termed poetic, often between inverted commas) we might as well discard huge sections of world literature, including most of what comes within the precincts of tragedy.

Many teachers would reject the idea of using pulp fiction as teaching material because it is below the standards that they want to sow their students. So, now and then, a moral factor creeps in through the back door. However, it should not be forgotten that several works from earlier centuries that are acknowledged as serious literature, even masterpieces, by modern critics contain more than a handful of 'popular' ingredients – Dickens novels provide a storehouse of examples. And Charlotte Brontë's *Jane Eyre* would – admittedly in an abridged version – qualify for acceptance by any weekly magazine.

As a matter of fact, from a pedagogical point of view, much popular literature is not without some assets: the characters undergo little or no development, which means that the stories can prompt profitable discussions about the difference between types and individuals and between heroes and villains in literature. The predictability of the plot naturally leads to an analysis of narrative structure as such: what are the building blocks of a story, what factors contribute to keeping the ball rolling, in what way or ways can an incident be brought to an end, etc. Perhaps the most rewarding field of research is the language: what makes the setting so stereotyped, what knee-jerk associations does the writer hope to trigger off in the reader in the description of the protagonist and his status symbols, etc.

Some of the features mentioned in the previous paragraph would seem to make popular literature suited for a beginners' course because things are presented openly, so to speak. However, there are pedagogic liabilities as well. In a very general way it can be said that popular fiction offers little scope for explanations and discussions because it chooses to concentrate on carefully selected 'slices of life': the setting is little more than a sterile background decoration, and work is seen by the characters in terms of a prestige symbol, or as a place where it is possible to meet 'interesting people'. What is more, it is taken for granted that all problems have clear-cut solutions, and the difficulties that loom large in the early stages of the story are not resolved thanks to any inherent logic, but rather as the result of a sudden and basically inexplicable transformation, or by what may be called a *deus ex machina* axe stroke.

Experience shows that, no matter how rewarding popular literature may be in some respects, students will soon get tired of it (the question whether valuable literature tires students has never been properly investigated!): the fact that is has a narrow scale of values, treating issues of life and death at the same level as housewives' quandaries allows for little classroom discussion. Even more importantly, its predictable pattern prevents it from accepting and reflecting the amorphous dynamism of life. And one component of what is called value seems to be a text's willingness to accept, and ability to cope with, at least some of those challenges. A linguistic analysis might take its starting-point in the stereotyped vocabulary of most popular literature.

Texts with a propaganda bias belong in the same category as popular literature: some features may be interesting to look at, in this case the writer's use of language. The teacher's hope is that an analysis of the language may put the students on their guard against some politicians' and demagogues' misuse of the medium.

Can psychology be of any use in the attempt to isolate texts that are suitable teaching material? Psychologists could be imagined to tell us what kind of texts are 'good' or 'less good', or even 'bad', for people to concern themselves with.

The American psychologist Daniel E. Berlyne (1924–76) has some pertinent things to say in this respect.[11] As he sees it, what prompts reaction in a person (or, in his terminology, what drives arousal to higher levels) is preoccupation with objects that are by their nature varied and diverse. What is complex and heterogeneous incites us because, potentially, it creates a conflict. The point is to avoid extremes, i.e. the unnecessarily complicated or the totally uniform, for such objects confuse and frustrate us.[12] What causes pleasure is the golden mean between factors that produce arousals and factors that allay arousal. The important thing is to keep arousal within bounds, and that containment is brought about by one or more organizing factors.

Even if Berlyne's theories may, to some extent, be a reflection of the 'spirit' of the 20th century – the New Critics were concerned with irony and paradox – they do have some applicability outside philosophy. Berlyne's thesis is that if we want to activate e.g. students, we should choose texts that are complex, but not so complex as to be unintelligible. The ordering factors in a literary work that prevent arousal going berserk are the author's command of the language and his alternations between tempting the reader onwards and disappointing his expectations.

However, some reservations will have to be made to a wholesale pedagogic applicability of Berlyne's theories: every teacher knows that banal and straightforward texts may prompt at least some arousal because they rarely fail to provoke readers possessed of a minimum of maturity. Secondly, texts whose complexity is not altogether eliminated by a state of balance – e.g. texts that do not reach an immediately satisfactory solution – are often highly suitable when it comes to raising the level of activity. For 'appropriate' texts need not be provided with a happy ending or suggest clear-cut solutions, but they must be the drop of water that somehow mirrors the universe. And life does not always provide the answers. That is what makes the so-called absurd dramatists excellent teaching material. It is true that they contain little or no action, but they do have something fundamental to say about the way people talk to each other and behave towards each other when they are having, or believe themselves to be having, their backs to the wall. And the point is that the language they use is perfectly comprehensible.

Comprehensibility – sheer understanding of the language and content of a text – is of course of decisive importance. it is not advisable to try and ram Joyce's *Ulysses* down the throats of beginners. Difficult words, convoluted syntax and foggy presentation do not make for easy reading. It is bad when the medium blocks the way of the message. On the other hand, Joyce's collection of short stories called *Dubliners* is a model classroom text: the stories are fascinating and open the gates of numerous pedagogic activities.

In a general way, it can be said that especially two types of text are serviceable, viz. those that take their starting-point in topical or current events and make use of them to illustrate eternal truths: Hemingway's novel *A Farewell to Arms* describes vividly the horror and meaninglessness of the First World War, but, over and above that, the book teaches us something essential about human beings. The book is instructive in that it brings some values up for discussion.

The second criterion of eligibility is the extent to which it is possible for the recipients to identify with or distance themselves from the problems or the characters of the text. Children feel pleasure when reading or listening to exciting stories. Quite spontaneously, they side with, indeed sometimes they 'are', the hero who courageously and successfully fights the villain. Golding's *Lord of the Flies* is a sure winner because the three boys, Ralph, Piggy, and Jack, are not only recognizable individuals whom the reader may like or dislike. More than that, they epitomize three distinct and different philosophies of life and attitudes to society. Furious discussions arise when the teacher asks the students to imagine what would happen if the three characters had been girls.

It is a truism in all teaching that the movement should be from the simple towards the more complex, but the truism requires some modification. For one thing, this is obviously not the way children learn their native language: they pick up bits here and there and gradually gain control. Secondly, it is a remarkable fact that readers of all ages are prepared to go to considerable lengths to get to grips with a text which, for some reason, captivates them. They do not mind 'standing on tiptoe', and aesthetic experience is not contingent on full understanding of all details.

This question of engagement also applies to the teacher. One answer to the question of what texts a teacher is to use might therefore be that he is to teach the literature of which he feels that he can be an advocate – sometimes an *advocatus diaboli*. It hardly needs adding that the teacher's sense of responsibility (and curriculum requirements) should tell him when to dismount his hobby horse. A good teacher will so arrange his material that he never loses sight of his students, literally as well as figuratively speaking. And he will know how to change gear when the expression of their eyes is becoming too bewildered, or when their yawning is becoming too audible.

Contemporary literature is good for beginners because the frame of reference will largely coincide with that of the reader, who can pretty easily decode the signals of the text. But at some point in their study, students should be made familiar with the pathfinders of earlier ages as well. It may be a useful eye opener for 21st century students to read Romantic texts, in which nature is seen as a pure and wellnigh divine force; or Neo-Classical texts with their predilection for rules and imitation. Understanding such texts may counteract the ahistoricism which is one of the scourges of our own age. Another instance of the didactic usefulness of literature.

It hardly needs saying that it is imperative to read texts dealing with other age groups and social classes than those to which the students themselves belong. That may be an efficient cure against the narcissism which is a prevalent feature of 'the spirit of our age'.

All genres offer suitable material, but not to the same extent, and not at the same level. Undoubtedly, many teachers will have found that non-fiction presents more difficulties in a classroom than even fairly complicated poems. The reason is that even an obscure poem may contain a paraphrasable core, a recognizable story that can be debated. A non-fiction text, on the other hand, is often a long chain of argumentation; even if concrete examples may occur, the overall thought is frequently abstract, and it requires a considerable amount of concentration to follow the writer's reasoning throughout the text.

The literature that is taught should be the real thing. That may be an ideal that is sometimes difficult to achieve in the case of beginners, but at all levels the teacher must be on his guard against shallow abridgements and aesthetically inferior adaptations. Novels, for example, always lose part of their flavour – sometimes of their organic coherence – by being served in extracts. The teacher should always remember that increasing maturity in his students is accompanied by an increasing awareness of quality.

Good texts give occasion to varied work forms, and sometimes also to reinterpretations of the conventional distribution of roles between teacher and student. Accordingly, preoccupation with literature is important not only for the result it achieves, but also for the intellectual processes that it inspires.

CHAPTER FIVE

The Teacher

The teacher is a specialist of his subject, just as a doctor and a lawyer are of theirs. No matter what teaching method is adopted, the responsibility for what goes on during the individual sessions as well as for the result of a possible examination is ultimately his. His greater knowledge and experience makes him an authority. The teacher of literature is supposed to sharpen his critical intelligence by getting steeped in literature and by familiarizing himself with what competent people have said or written about individual works as well as about more theoretical problems.

For even if the demands put on teacher of literature are, to a very large extent, identical with those facing a teacher of any other subject, there are some marked differences. 'Understanding' a literary text it not the same thing as 'understanding' a mathematical formula. But the teacher of literature's pedagogic talent manifests itself not least in the degree of competence with which he adapts his own opinions and impressions of a given work to the backgrounds of the students he is in charge of. A good reader of literature should be able to identify with another human being's situation, and similarly a good teacher of literature should have, or develop, a sure instinct for where students are likely to have difficulties. The leaps of abstraction required in a math problem are not identical with those required in the case of literature. In math, the usual situation for answers is either right or wrong. Not so where literature is concerned. Here, a 100% correct answer is difficult to obtain.

The teacher's task is a truly formidable one: he must be conversant with literature as such, and its artistic effects; he must have the pedagogic competence that enables him to envisage a suitable method of dealing with the day's text, and he must have the human experience and breadth of vision that permits him to be responsible to the work without mauling the text or regimenting his students. It is his obvious duty to fill lacunae in the students' knowledge and to furnish them with background information in the case of an author, a theme, or a literary movement. And his students should not be given the impression that he is carrying on a dialogue with the text over their heads.

'Doing' literature means, to a great extent, becoming aware of, and trying to formulate, a series of questions. The fascination is that a good many of the questions can be answered in various ways, and that some of them are not susceptible of any final solution. That allows for a considerable amount of freedom – freedom to say relevant and intelligent as well as decidedly irrelevant and unintelligent things about a text, but also a kind of freedom that is not unlimited. The good teacher is the man or woman who can walk that tightrope without falling off. The teacher should never overestimate his students' knowledge, and never underestimate their desire to acquire more knowledge.

Literature is more than a mush of muddled feelings; the teaching of it is an intellectual pursuit. However, even if precision is desirable, the ethical aspect implied should not be ignored. The teacher should show the same degree of tact as he will do in any two-way communication from which he intends to derive some benefit. Literature is not a mechanical string of words, and reading literature usually influences students profoundly; the teaching of it may radically alter the standards the students carry with them, indeed their whole view of life. Hence, the teacher should use some caution in the pressure he brings to bear on his students to prompt reactions on their part. The teacher should be aware that, when teaching literature, he is likely to provoke very strong feelings in the recipients, some of whom will feel deeply engaged in the text and have formed their own opinion, so the gamut will stretch from indignation to strong empathy. Such reactions are often difficult to defuse, and virtually impossible to programme.

A teacher should be wary of dismissing out of hand suggestions or interpretations that differ from his own. After some moment's reflection or a proper classroom discussion they may turn out to be not so foolish at all. The more experienced a teacher becomes, the more he will be incline to agree with T.S. Eliot, who said about the criticism of literature that there is no one method, but varying degrees of human experience. That statement applies *mutatis mutandis*, to a classroom situation as well. Ideally, stepwise progression goes hand in hand with increasing demands for precision. One of the tricks of the teacher's trade is to learn how to build on his students' contributions and gently lead them towards a greater and richer understanding and, hopefully, enjoyment. The fullness of the experience is in direct proportion to the number of nuances that are incorporated. Sometimes the really Big Questions concerning life and death are at stake.

One of the aims of literary pedagogy is to make the students better readers, which more than anything else means making them sensitive to the writer's use of language. Unfortunately, there is little research into what high-level reading means.[1] And a teacher will soon discover that literacy is not equally distributed among mankind. Some guesses are more informed than others. The fullness of the experience is proportional to the number of nuances that are incorporated. Some kind of 'rounding off' is imperative at all levels, but it is rarely advisable to size up a book with statements like 'Well it's really nothing but . . . '

The teacher's qualifications are determined by his personal background and his professional competence. It is a well-known fact that professional competence is an indispensable requisite of good pedagogy. Also, he should master different teaching techniques. But, over and above all that, he should have, or develop, a talent for social interaction, i.e. the way he plays his part in the noble game of teaching that he and the recipients are engaged in.

The teacher should be able to establish a good atmosphere. Some of the components of that somewhat fluid concept would seem to be the following: (1) mutual confidence. The students must feel that they can rely not only on the teacher's professional competence, but also on his conduct. They must be made to feel that they are in good hands. Freakish behaviour in a classroom is counterproductive, and irony should always be directed towards somebody or something outside the classroom, *never* towards one of the students. (2) motivation for the day's work; if the teacher is entirely devoid of *engagement*, he cannot hope to inspire his students with any enthusiasm. (3) respect for the ongoing process. On this point, too, the indirect teaching, viz. the example set by the teacher, is of paramount importance. If the teacher is constantly badly prepared or patently uninterested (yawning, body language, forgotten his books), or if it is evident that he has no plan at all for 'what is going to happen next', he cannot expect his collaborators to pick up the fragments.

The teacher's situation is the opposite of his students': his job is to 'break down' his own interpretation of a given text and arrange it in portions that can be consumed by his audience – meet them where they stand, but certainly not leave them there. However, it is no easy matter to combine the openness and receptivity that are a *sine qua non* in textual analysis. There will inevitably be sudden glimpses of inspiration from one or more members of the group, short circuits, and repetitions, leaps forwards and backwards. Accordingly, the teacher's plan should be flexible, allowing room for improvisations and digressions (which latter are, as we all know, the sunshine of life). Digressions may be good starters: if one of the participants brings up a question which is, at first glance, off the point, it may still captivate the other members of the learning community and cause them to forget that, actually, we are not moving strictly according to the original outline. That means that the teacher's plan for the lesson will have to include a certain amount of flexibility.

The better the teacher is prepared, the greater are the chances of a successful lesson; the more suitable a text is, the more smoothly things are likely to proceed; the greater the teacher's knack is of coping with unexpected situations (which show an uncanny tendency of invariably cropping up!), the better will he be able to establish a smoothly-working cooperation. Presence of mind is one of the cardinal virtues of a teacher; it enables him to adjust the speed of the process to the students' response, and to round it off if, for some reason, the text misfires.

It is incumbent on the teacher to show that learning does not necessarily have to be a burdensome duty, but that it is perfectly compatible with a considerable amount of satisfaction. In blissful moments, the teacher may get the impression that the learning process is carried on by its own impetus even if the conductor has lowered his baton Everybody shares the feeling that 'we are hunting big game together'. But then again, of course the teacher should be willing to listen to his students' suggestions and objections, but also to call a halt if he can see that they are just marking time. The teacher's greater knowledge and experience makes him an authority – it does not have to make him authoritarian. Thus, he should not shy away from saying, 'You may not be able to see the immediate applicability of the aspect we are talking about, but it is necessary for you to familiarize yourselves with it before you are able to proceed with the text'. On the other hand, he will weaken his position if his standard answer too often is: 'Well, I'm at a loss here. Your guess is as good as mine'. Informed guesses may be productive, especially if they *are* informed.

Another aim is to make the students as articulate and exact as possible. That means that the teacher will not infrequently be forced to stretch a safety net under such students as have little or no feeling for literature. Here, the acceptance of different thresholds of interpretation comes in.[2] A reader of literature should be able to understand, perhaps identify, with another human being's situation, and similarly a good teacher should have, or develop, an instinctive feeling for where the students are likely to have difficulties.

All the time, the teacher, besides being a participant, will also be an observer of the progress of events. He may hope to find himself in a state of ecstasy in the Greek sense of the word: 'the state of rapture in which the soul, liberated from the body, was engaged in the contemplation of divine things' (OED). Ideally, he makes a mental list of his own procedures' and methods' successes and failures for later use.

The sublime teacher is capable of paying attention to the learning process that is going on before his eyes and, at the same time, placing himself outside the proceedings, observing, reflecting, and concluding.

CHAPTER SIX
The Reader

The be-all and end-all of serious work with literature is careful, successive perusals of the text that is going to be analysed. It is an illusion to believe that one reading will ensure safe and reliable navigation in a literary universe.

The reader who appears in these pages is the human being whom the author addresses in the hope of finding, or creating, a kindred spirit, a person who is willing to suspend his disbelief and join the game in which the author asks him to participate, a supportive, but not uncritical cooperator. That is what is meant by 'the reader' in this chapter. On the analogy of the term 'implied author', we might call him 'implied reader'.

A poem, for example, is not a haphazard hodge-podge of typographical signs, but a structure organized in accordance with certain conventions. The reader is the person who has (or is given, e.g. through teaching) some talents enabling him or her to decode the signals of the structure and establish a dialogue with the text. That means that certain demands are made on the reader for the cooperation between himself, the text, and the author to succeed.

The reader knows intuitively that a word only acquires meaning when placed in a context; but he also knows that a word in a text will become significant the moment it is grasped as a balance between itself and the whole of the text. The cooperation between words and sentences creates expectations in the reader – expectations that are continuously modified. Each word, sentence, paragraph, chapter etc. has a series of potentialities that are confirmed or denied by what went before and what follows. Reading is both a backward-looking and a forward-looking process. The question of parts versus wholes becomes relevant here: it is impossible to read both a part and the whole at the same time. As Professor Nordhjem points out, all understanding proceeds gradually. Chapter One throws light on Chapter Two, but Chapter Two may also, in its turn, throw a new light on Chapter One. A passage acquires more depth the further we read on.[1]

The reader must know the language of the text, but also some of the norms and conventions that make the text comprehensible. He understands how events can be linked together and grouped, and in what way or ways a text can be rounded off. With more advanced experience, he comes to possess a sense of what incidents in a text are the really important ones, and which of them can be subsumed under others. He will also comprehend the fact that some incidents exist in their own right and, at the same time, point beyond themselves to something that is different, perhaps greater and more general, than they are in themselves, i.e. he is capable of seeing some items in the text as symbols. Gradually it will become clear to him what are the problems presented by a text, and what, if any, the solutions – which may sometimes point to issues that are to be found outside the universe of the text.

The reader's progressive understanding permits him to make a synthesis of the material so that a universe with people, localities, forces and feelings is created. He integrates individual words and sentences into a larger framework of time and space. He will be able to fill in what seems to him to be lacunae in the material. What is hinted or implied is no less important than what is explicitly stated, indeed sometimes the content of a text may change its character once some implications have been brought to light. Occasionally, a text may be comparable to an iceberg of which only the tip is visible. When the behavior of a character in a novel seems incomprehensible, it may be a hidden invitation to the reader to supplement such connecting links as will make sense of the character's words and acts. Sometimes the teacher must be prepared to point to some stepping-stones, for lacunae may often be structurally meaningful.

Reading is not only a matter of accumulating some items, but also of making them into a system. In the process, the reader makes use of some of the procedures that are used in situations outside literature: generalization, abstraction, induction, deduction, hypothesis, conclusion, etc. Understanding a text is an operation the goal of which is to grasp the near-totality of it. That is why repeated readings are necessary to explore, but not necessarily empty, the polysemy of the text. No reader can aspire to get an indisputably complete grasp of a fictional text,[2] but without undue raising of forefingers it may be pointed out that some things in a text may reward a re-reading.

All works cannot be read in the same way. Dryden's *Ode on St, Cecilia's Day* requires a different reading from a story by Somerset Maugham. Accordingly, the teaching of literature should also include the teaching of different reading techniques. Every reader will have experienced that some texts do not open up immediately, but the blame should not always be placed at the author's door. The text and the teacher prepare the material, and the latter does his best to remove possible obstacles, but the final leap – from reading via understanding to enjoyment – is the sole responsibility of the recipient. Often a student's understanding is reflected not only in his words (e.g. the answers he gives), but also in his body language, and his eyes may express awareness, pleasure, relief – even thankfulness.

Most people are familiar with the drawing that can 'be' both a duck and a rabbit, depending on the way in which it is viewed. Examples of such drawings are legion, and they are interesting because the same objectively given form is susceptible of radically different interpretations, but also because looking at a form implies trying to interpret it. That is why modern theories of reading tend to emphasize the reader's active role in the process in that he is held to be not only the decoder of the text, but also, to some extent, the encoder. That is where the Reader Response critics took their cue. While reading, the reader will all the time have to perform a series of mental operations, such as making and revising suppositions. And the result of what the reader 'reads into' the text will inevitably be coloured by factors in his own mind. The implied reader responds to the text.

Interest in the recipient's response is as old as criticism itself. According to Aristotle, the purpose of tragedy is to establish *katharsis*, or purification, in the spectator. Thanks to its plot, the drama is to "affect through pity and terror the correction and refinement of such passions".[3] Horace's statement that literature is to *prodesse et delectare* (i.e. give instruction and delight) as well as Longinus' reflections on sublimity show that they wanted to include the reader's reactions in their criteria of a successful work of art.

Every teacher knows that students who have read very little may turn out to be excellent readers even if they may be missing the tools to verbalize their experience, which means that their formulations may be tentative and groping On the other hand, people at advanced levels who have read heaps of books may be mediocre readers. Both categories present fascinating challenges to the teacher.

The implied reader is no identifiable person.[4] He has got neither personal nor social attributes, but he is characterized by the way in which he agrees to play the part of the cooperative participant, i.e. to follow, in a sympathetic spirit, the guidelines laid down by the author in the text. He must train his memory and possess no little talent of combination. It is within the reach of virtually anybody to become at least an acceptable implied reader, and one of the noblest purposes of literary pedagogy is to lead him gently on the way.

CHAPTER SEVEN
The Workshop

Interpretation

A dog's tail usually hangs limply, so when he begins to wag it, our spontaneous conclusion is that the movement of his tail must mean something. This intuitive reading a meaning into an observation is interpretation. Since a dog wags his tail when he sees his master or is invited to go for a walk, but never when he growls or bites, we want to find an explanation of his changing behaviour, and, again intuitively, we characterize – interpret – his conduct by an analogy from our world and conclude that the pattern of behaviour is a sign of satisfaction or pleasure. We place the dog's wagging in a human context even if we do not know whether he actually does feel happy the way a human being does. As we see tail-wagging in similar circumstances in all dogs, we ascribe general validity to our conclusion: tail-wagging is a sign of satisfaction in dogs.

Interpretation, then, is basically man-centred, or anthropocentric. It is a tribute to man's rational faculties because it does not question the capacity of the human brain to encompass and explain most of what happens in books and in the universe as well as in man's own mind. Interpretation is an attempt to find a rational explanation of something that may baffle us at first sight, to challenge and defeat the incomprehensibility of the world we live in. The human brain interprets incessantly and at full throttle to make sense of the world. What we consider a successful interpretation gives us a comforting feeling because it is based on the assumption that things that seem to be 'outside' man are explicable within his terms of reference, and that the world is characterized by comprehensibility, perhaps even a pattern of regularity.

Interpretation takes place within all spheres of life: soothsayers have taken the way birds fly to have relevance for aspects of human life, and astrologers point out the importance of the movements and relative positions of the celestial bodies for what happens on earth. Some people tend to shake their heads at the activities of soothsayers and astrologers, because, to them, interpretation is more than a hobby or a ritual exercise. It is a reflection of man's need to feel that he controls the universe by understanding it, and of his suborn efforts to control 'reality'. We all feel uncomfortable when faced with something we cannot make sense of. Phenomena of some complexity as well as symbolic objects urge man to attempt to make sense of them. We need only think of the system of symbols called language, which is the subject of a permanent process of interpretation.

The human need of explaining and 'taming' is just as great in literary texts as where the position of the planets is concerned. That is why the discipline of textual interpretation is as old as the history of the written text. Biblical exegesis is a case in point. From time immemorial, man has desired to place the problem of a text within a framework that he is familiar with.

In a teaching situation, interpretation is usually required not only to ensure understanding, but also to pave the way for what is called the literary experience. Of course students are to be made familiar with the pleasure of reading a good text. But in order to obtain such pleasure, they will benefit from getting to know aspects of the art of going 'into' and 'behind' a text. Indeed, what is called the literary experience is often the feeling or feelings accompanying the progressive, insight-expanding treatment of the text. That is not to say that a reader cannot be deeply moved by a text without being able to state what it 'signifies', and without being able to bring it into agreement with something he knows from 'the real world'. It is also true that a teacher who insists on a heavy-handed and mechanical 'emptying' of the text will do a lot of harm. However, the fact remains that the alternative to a teacher-assisted interpretation in the great majority of cases will turn out to be no interpretation. And where students of literature are concerned, it is absurd to leave them entirely to their own devices.

The Two Phases of Interpretation

There are two stages in textual interpretation, viz. establishing meaning (i.e. answering the question 'What does the text say?') and transforming meaning into significance (i.e. answering the question 'What picture of reality is given here?'). The art of understanding and the art of interpreting are two functions, but in our 'classroom' case either of them presupposes the other. In Bourdieu's words, to understand understanding is to realize why some tradition attached to a universe that is more or less distant from our own in time and space should address us in a language we more or less wholly share.[1] The structuralists put it in the following way: understanding a text means becoming able to throw light on a series of significant structures that are 'given' in a work. Interpreting a text is putting this sum of structures into a context, i.e. a larger, surrounding structure. The latter may be our world, but it may also be the author's life, or the age in which he lived.

We might illustrate the two functions with the aid of an ancient analogy: we are to be both the traveller who experiences the landscape here and now, and the cartographer who contemplates the landscape from a temporal and spatial distance.

What Does the Text Say?

On the face of it, it would seem to be fairly simple for a reader to find out what a text says, provided, of course, that he knows the language in which it is written. However, on closer inspection, it turns out that there are considerable difficulties involved.

Language is a dubious friend rather than a trustworthy ally. As F. R. Leavis pointed out, a work is a meeting-place of minds.[2] Language is not 'one-dimensional', and it is a wrong assumption that language generally renders facts. It is only in a very few cases, such as mathematics and chemistry that language has only denotational value. The speech acts theorists stressed the importance of the illocutionary force of most messages, which means that there is more in a statement than mere semantic meaning: most texts are open to interpretation.

Secondly, the picture of reality that a literary text gives is not a photographic likeness: it is fiction (Bourdieu's 'second world'), which means that it is not objectively true. Indeed, many literary texts make a point of not being literally true.

Thirdly, from the beginning of the reading process the reader is bound to run into the so-called hermeneutic dilemma. Hermeneutics is the science of interpretation, and the sticking-point is, to put it briefly and paradoxically, that any understanding presupposes understanding. The interrelation of wholes and parts is relevant here: in order to understand e.g. the game of football, you must have some 'Vorverständnis', i.e. 'before-understanding', as German hermeneutics calls it. You must know what is meant by foul play, goal, corner, etc. to see the meaning of the play. But you must also understand the meaning of the whole play of which those items are constituent parts. You cannot know the true meaning of a part without knowing the whole of which is it a part. But then again, the whole is the sum of the parts, which means that it is influenced by its components. Accordingly you do not know the quality of the whole without knowing the true meaning of the parts. Your understanding of a text proceeds as a continuous shuttling between the parts and the whole, which mutually explain and illuminate each other. In the process, you establish hypotheses, which are confirmed or denied as your reading continues. In cases where a hypothesis is disproved, it will have to be adjusted, or perhaps rejected, which, incidentally, is not as simple as it may sound.

When you begin to 'get into' a text, you will soon discover that you will have to incorporate material from outside the text: if you do not, you will not get anywhere. And there is another complication: all experience goes to show that our initial overall impression of a text forms the basis of what we later 'understand' in the text. What we find is, to a large extent, determined by what we expect to find. We are influenced by what psychologists call 'confirmation bias'. It takes a considerable intellectual effort to alter a first impression. One of the characteristics of a good reader is that he masters such an operation.

Literary Competence

When dealing with a text, the reader brings to bear more than mere linguistic competence, viz. something that might be termed 'general knowledge'. Human beings have consciousness, they can think, feel, speak, act; life and death have the same meaning in literature as they have in life; the same goes for truth and falsehood. Logic is respected, e.g. in the sense that an act is usually followed by consequences. And our criteria for estimating people's behaviour in a text derive from the standards of our own world: literature copies life.

But perhaps there is more to it than that. In her novel *The Prime of Miss Jean Brodie* Muriel Spark lets the eccentric teacher Jean Brodie say, "The word 'education' comes from the root *e*, from *ex*, and *duco*, I lead. It means a leading out. To me education is leading out of what is already there in the pupil's soul."[3] Miss Brodie has probably noticed that most of her pupils have got a certain understanding of some aspects of literature without anything having been put in their heads. She seems to presuppose that there is such a thing as an innate sense of literature.

The theory of literary competence inspired the American sociologist Noam Chomsky's reflections on 'linguistic competence': if we want to understand how language is acquired and used, he says, we must presuppose a cognitive system that 'is there' from the beginning and is developed in early childhood, a linguistic ability which is at the basis of our behaviour, but which is not describable in simple behaviorist models or an easily comprehensible stimulus–response psychology.[4] Chomsky was struck by a person's ability to express thoughts that had never been expressed before, and to understand thoughts that had never been verbalized before. He was confident that it must be due to the existence of some mechanisms – he does not specify what types they are – that generate knowledge of language. The sum of those mechanisms is what he calls linguistic competence.

He postulates that the human mind is possessed of

an innate talent, viz. that of mastering a universal grammar. It is latent in all people, but manifests itself differently, depending on the language in which the child is brought up.

It is not difficult to point out weaknesses in Chomsky's postulate. The ontological status of his 'deep structure' remains dubious, which made it vulnerable in an age that preferred empirical evidence. Also, many of the operations within his 'transformation grammar' as his system came to be called, are not convincingly argued. However, the fact remains that even a 7-year old child will be able to use grammatically correct structures which he cannot possibly have heard before. And the fact also remains that a really satisfactory explanation of that phenomenon is still missing.

'Literary competence' is, at best, a fluid designation. If it is taken to mean that some people are more qualified than others to pass sentence on things literary, it is a commonplace that tells us nothing we did not know. Besides, experience shows that a person does not need to have a formal literary training in order to give perspicacious assessments of literary phenomena in the widest sense of the word. And perhaps we should leave that idea of 'competence' at that.

If, however, the 'competence' refers to an innate talent, shared by humanity at large, things begin to become metaphysical. It seems to be a fact that the great majority of men and women, also untutored people, are able, intuitively, to identify a text as fiction, and to distinguish between fiction and non-fiction. Most people will be able to understand when e.g. a novel is rounded off. Where does that ability come from? A literary work may have a number of different meanings, but not *any* meaning. How come? How do we explain the fact that some readings are, by general consensus, better than others? Literary competence must be constituted in such a way that it is not identical down to the smallest detail in all human beings, for we can have widely different legitimate understandings of the same text.

Literature makes use of many of the effects that all people are familiar with from their daily lives: rhythm, repetitions, control, expectation, so literature depends on life. Children know literature when they begin to know something about life. Is it all bound up with man's capacity to tell 'reality' from 'non-reality'? An answer to that question will only take us any further if we also try to account for such a capacity. Miss Brodie did not pursue the point, but we could at least try to use it as a discussion topic with the students.

Any teacher will of course be pleased when he realizes that 'there is something to build on', and everything seems to prove that the experience that literature gives its readers is contingent on his linguistic and literary 'preparedness', which again illustrates the importance of inviting and inspiring students to read as many literary works as possible. But mankind is not composed of literary scholars *in embryo.*

Getting to Grips with the Text

Analysis procedures change from one text to another, but also from one group of students to another. A competent teacher will soon detect that aggregate of attitudes, intelligence, receptivity, and willingness to cooperate and join the game which may be subsumed under the designation 'the identity of the group'. There are imponderables in all teaching: two treatments of the same work in two groups at the same level are rarely, if ever, identical. When the teacher speaks *ex cathedra,* it is possible to practise 'programmed revelation'. On the other hand, if more initiative is left to members of the group, more 'hit-and-miss' incidents are inevitable.

Imagination

Like the world in Shakespeare's *The Merry Wives of Windsor* (I,2,2) the text is an oyster, and the point is to find one or more efficient 'swords' to open it. But it is impossible to start your reading from scratch. The majority of students are surprised when they are told that it is an illusion to believe that you can tackle a text from a Lockean *tabula rasa* stage. We agree on the way the words are to be read, but implications and associations, the whole mental set-up, will be coloured by the reader's own background. That goes for knowledge, experience, intuition, and imagination. Often the difficulty of assessing what is and what is not in a text is bound up with the part played by the imagination. The reason is that any text contains 'empty spaces' ('three days later'), which readers at different levels of maturity tackle differently. Every teacher of literature will know that what are called 'unacceptable' interpretations may be based on actually erroneous readings of the text; but in a good many instances an absurd interpretation is caused by the reader's imagination running riot.

Imagination may be a faithful servant, but an insidious master. A reader's imagination should be trained to work *with* the text, i.e. in continuation or elaboration of it, and not *against* it or *beside* it, as the Deconstructionists often do. The type of imagination that teaching should inspire is *fertile* and at the same time *disciplined.* Fertile because a dull and humdrum handling of the text will never be able to do justice to what is happening in the literary universe. The task of the imagination is to put the suggestions and implications of the text in a larger context. On the other hand, a string of airy postulates that use the text as a launch pad for idiosyncratic and largely unfounded conclusions rarely makes anyone wiser, for which reason it is a good thing to give students some very elementary rules to guide them in their process of 'imagining'. For instance, the teacher might suggest that, in the day's text, irony is a good angle of approach; or he may ask the students to look at the relationship between content and form; or he might suggest that a sonnet is rarely a social pamphlet, etc. The relationship between the work and the reader's imagination can be compared to that existing between a boy and the paper kite he is flying: it should be given the opportunity of soaring, but, thanks to the string, the boy will always be able to pull it back to earth.

Western thinking is, basically, characterized linear progression. However, ground-breaking scientific discoveries were made by men and women who did not follow the beaten track but had a glimpse of imaginative insight, perhaps a caprice or sudden impulse that they decided to pursue. Are such epiphanies evidence that there is a Great Something behind what we see, feel, and think? A kind of Ultimate Reality which our daily routine prevents us from apprehending? The thought might give credence to something reminiscent of an innate literary competence, for how else do we explain alternative visions?

We are moving in a pedagogic minefield here. How valuable is it to postulate connections that nobody has so far been able to see? The history of criticism contains numerous examples of individual observations and 'total' interpretations that were ignored or denounced as beside the point when published, but which later rose to great honour. One might point to the New Critics' discovery and reappraisal of the 'metaphysical poets' of the 17th century. Add to this, it is the imaginative people that cause the world to move, not the over-cautious philistines. Consequently, teaching should inspire an open and imagination-friendly attitude to textual work.

It is never a wise policy to reject out of hand a suggestion that seems at first sight to be untenable. But then again, the point of Wordsworth's *Tintern Abbey* is not to give a topographically correct description of the landscape.

Paraphrase

A paraphrase ('retelling the content in our own words') is a useful device to make a text more manageable; the aim is to facilitate the students' broad idea of the text. It does that by contributing to setting up the literary universe because it clarifies the distinction between the textual and the extra-textual context. Moreover, since it is obviously beside the point to include everything in such an account, it makes it easier for the student to separate the wheat from the chaff: what is significant and what is trivial? It may even suggest the relationship that exists between the parts and the whole. A prose paraphrase of a poem can be valuable in that it helps to pin down some of the factors that make up 'the poetry' of the text. A poem is rarely translatable into other languages, but a paraphrase of it, as of many other literary texts, will be. A paraphrase is also susceptible of translation into other media: screen versions of novels are usually loyal to the broad outlines of the plot whereas they tend to treat the minutiae more perfunctorily.

Paraphrases are not equally suitable to all types of text: static and descriptive passages (landscapes, meditations) are difficult to paraphrase. In such cases, the function of a paraphrase can be to simplify the syntax of the text and 'translate' its vocabulary.

The paraphrase is not an evaluation of the text, not a characterization of its participants, not a discussion of its assumptions, and not just a more or less judicious selection of the words of the text connected with a chain of 'and then's'. A paraphrase does not interpret. One of the most difficult things to teach students is to avoid interpreting when paraphrasing.

The paraphrase has one evident pedagogic advantage, viz. that it offers slow students the opportunity of saying at least something about a text. However, a teacher will soon find out that it is no easy matter for everybody to 'say the same thing in other words'. Philosophers and linguists are doubtful whether it is actually possible to express the same thought in several different ways. And many students are likely to exclaim,"But that's what it says in the text!" when confronted with a paraphrase. As a matter of fact, a considerable amount of practice is needed before some students get the hang of the technique and purpose of the paraphrase.

There are several types of paraphrase: the detailed one that follows all the meanderings of the text, which is practicable (and practical!) with many poems and complicated prose contexts; another type, the summary, condenses a long text to some main points (suitable in the case of long texts), and finally the 'nutshell' paraphrase, very often little more than a list of key words from the text. It is serviceable with scenes of a drama and chapters of a novel.

Digging Deeper

With an average group, it is possible to get beyond the paraphrase stage with practically all the students, but all experience shows that the great majority of students need a helping (sometimes loving!) hand if they are to get a life-size portrait of the text. The paraphrase is, figuratively speaking, only a pit stop in our journey into unknown, but tempting, territory. Here are a few suggestions as to how to get on: it is always a good idea to examine the relationship between the title and the content of a text. What expectations are aroused in the reader when he reads the title of Philip Larkin's poem *Church Going*? In shorter texts, like many poems, a dividend-paying gambit is to watch the tenses of the verbs and the (changing) forms of the pronouns, especially where and why they change. How is tense used to render time? Who is the first-person 'I' of a Romantic poem? In a drama, the characters' entries and exits are practically always significant, especially, of course, those of the hero and the villain. In a non-fiction text, attention should be paid to the transitions from one paragraph to the next, and the concomitant development of the argumentation. What would happen if we change the order of the paragraphs? In a novel, which is a network of complex structures, the hermeneutic dilemma poses itself acutely. A good starting-point is to observe the incidence of coincidences, which are the building blocks of the structure. Some linguistic markers are highly informative: thus, contrasts may give useful hints as to the structure of the text, e.g. now versus then, you versus I, away versus home, or, more specifically, still versus round as in D. H. Lawrence's poem *Kisses in the Train.*

After the paraphrase, three operations are useful with any text, viz. making observations, gathering and systematizing observations, and concluding on the basis of observations, i.e. a stepwise progression in the reader's dialogue with the text.

In the further stages of textual analysis, movements in two seemingly opposite direction supplement each other, viz. *expansion* and *concentration.* The expansion works towards larger units and overall structures: it will be preoccupied with the extent to which the text illustrates more than its own situation, e.g. a universal problem. Robert Frost's poem *The Road Not Taken* is a model example. However, the text also expands in the sense that it conveys a feeling of respect for the creative personality behind the text, indeed for the scope of the human intellect, as is seen in Pope's *Essay on Man*.

Expansion permits the students to elaborate on the text, but it should not be carried to such lengths that everything is connected with everything else. Extrapolations of the text can be admissible, especially of course, in the case of open-ended texts. Such texts sometimes seem to hold an appeal to the reader to venture beyond the final full stop. It hardly needs to be stressed that expansions are only valuable to the extent that they are firmly based on the signals given in the text: how can a person whom the text has provided with such qualities be imagined to develop when the curtain has fallen? What is a conceivable solution to the dilemma the story ends with? Even in texts that seem to be rounded off, the question 'What will the situation be like two years later?' sometimes pays off.

Expansion may also 'move backwards' in the sense that it can be rewarding to discuss what goes before e.g. the opening scene of a drama. That procedure is of course particularly appropriate with texts that begin 'in the middle of things', which dramas nearly always do. Or an expansion may be a digression from the text: 'What would have happened if the female protagonist had not received the fatal letter until the following day?'

Concentration manifests itself as absorption in the intellectual content of the text, and in what makes it something unique even if it is not an isolated phenomenon in the literatures of the world. Just as expansion is not tantamount to heaven-bound soaring, concentration is not synonymous with reduction. The great majority of literary works deserve a better fate than a sigh of resignation accompanied with the words, 'Well, actually, it is nothing but . . . ' The plots of many great 19th century novels can be summarized in approximately ten lines, but that is not all there is to be said about e.g. the multifarious variety of the Dickensian universe.

Both expansion and concentration work in the direction of greater abstraction. However, a text can be eminently readable – and suitable as a pedagogic object – even if it remains on a fairly concrete level. Orwell's novels are cases in point.

Description and *characterization* are on a higher level of abstraction: the students are required to 'stand outside' the text and largely use their own words when performing those operations. The pedagogic advantage is that the students' vocabulary will almost invariably be extended and his oral performance improved. Characterization generally occurs in the evaluation of works in their entirety, and in connection with the words and actions of fictional characters. The teacher will soon realize that the kind of abstraction required in a characterization may present some difficulty, especially to young students. It takes some degree of maturity to be able to move from the verbs of the text to the adjectives that are necessary in a characterization, i.e. that a person who says or does this or that can be labelled by this or that adjective.

Analysis regards the text as an object to be examined. We go deeply into or 'behind' the text. From a pedagogical point of view, an assignment like summarizing is a fairly unequivocal operation because the summary is firmly rooted in the words of the text, which a paraphrase is to a lesser degree. However, analysis rises above the text. It is largely independent of the exact wording, indeed, sometimes it has to change into an entirely different vocabulary, for which reason it must begin by specifying its object: do we want a closer look at the narrative pattern of a novel, at the technique of characterization (Dickens' novels would furnish a rich crop here), at the use of irregular verbs in a poem? Precision of that type is necessary if the students are to keep their heads above water.

Accordingly, the teacher will often find it time-saving to suggest some guidelines that may help the students to get off to a good start. For example, if the purpose is an analysis of the narrative pattern of a story, students can be asked to look at the alternations between elements of plot and elements of description, the time sequences (are they chronological, circular, disconnected, etc.?), the ending compared with the beginning, and the placing of a possible climax.

Commenting on and *discussing* connect incidents of the text, or frequently the whole of it, with something outside it. Informed discussion or comment presupposes a high degree of familiarity with the text, not only the visible items of it, but also the attitudes, ideas, thoughts, etc. underlying it. When students make comments, they measure the universe of the text by the standards of their own conceptual world, or, to put it differently, comments depend on the commentator's maturity.

Discussion should be used as a pedagogic instrument. In order to be able to discuss the message of a poem, it is not enough to clarify your own views about it. In addition, you must be prepared to listen to others, to make concessions, and allow yourself to be influenced, perhaps even persuaded. Once more, the didactic aspect of the teaching of literature comes to the fore. For literary discussions, like comments, invariably come to embrace argumentation as well. And as the discussion proceeds, hopefully it becomes evident that the aim is not to floor the fellow with whom you disagree. It is not a matter of 'victory' for any of the participants, but rather, in the words of Montaigne, to 'frotter et limer votre cervelle contre celle d'autruy', i.e. file your own brain on somebody else's.

In order to be able to *draw conclusions,* the students must be able to combine a series of items, e.g. stylistic features in a poem, to weigh pros and cons, and, as the expression suggests, to reach some kind of verdict. It is a satisfactory intellectual pursuit to move, in the company of a group of students, from observation to preliminary conclusions, and onwards towards a more general conclusion. The difficulties are anything but negligible, for the final conclusion is reached by raising abstraction to the second power, so to speak. And since that stage is, at the same time, the reward of hard work and sometimes the point that the students remember best, great attention should be paid to the form of it.

Language

Preoccupation with literature also trains students how to use language for various purposes. The snag is, of course, that language is also the medium in which we couch our interpretation. Thus, language becomes the tool as well as the object of analysis. Modern criticism claims that the individual work of art *is* its form. Every novel reader will have experienced the difficulty, indeed impossibility, of distinguishing between the story and the way it is told. Changes of form invariably lead to changes of content. The point becomes clear to students when they are asked to give a prose paraphrase of a poem and compare it with the poem such as the author created it: the poem *is* its form.

The coalescence of content of form becomes evident when we look at modern 'adaptations' of Shakespeare's plays. The formidable impact of his plays is created not least by his use of language. When modern film and stage directors change – 'bowdlerize' – his language to make it more 'modern' or less offensive, the action on the stage frequently becomes absurd.

In some types of text, the formal aspect is pedagogically instructive: sentimental novels and thrillers strive to obtain an effect by pointing emphatically to certain items and repeating the trick. There is an accumulation of effects that are, figuratively speaking, superimposed on the content. The phenomenon called suspense is an arrangement of the narrative sequence with the purpose of keeping the reader on tenterhooks. Suspense is a manageable thing to most students, and they like to point out the linguistic means used by the author to intensify tension.

Syntax is a fertile research field. For pedagogic purposes it is practical to divide it into three categories: choice of words (archaic, technical, foreign, etc.), form of words (Biblical or Shakespearean reminiscences like 'thou hast'), and combination of words (parataxis versus hypotaxis, convoluted sentences as in Lyly's *Euphues*). (See pp. 95 et seq.) Again, students need little encouragement to start gathering material on their own, and to attempt to clarify how predominant use of one or the other of the categories may eventually colour the final result of their interpretation.

Re-symbolization

The process of literary interpretation will be an analytical progression. The result of the interpretation will take the shape of a synthesis with a new meaning. First we decode the text, and then we re-symbolize it. Such re-symbolizations seem to have certain characteristics: they are organizing, abstracting, generalizing, and man-orientated. Paul Ricoeur said that we attempt to "lay bare the levels of meaning contained in the literal sense."[5] Unity is an important convention where interpretation is concerned. A poet, describing different experiences, may not want to gather and organize them. However, an interpreter does want to. A detail in a text may often be taken to be representative of a class: we see a character in some selected situations and, on that basis, we feel justified in giving a general characterization of that person's ethical standards. We tend to see texts as specific examples of more or less generalized instances of the ways in which man relates to the world. A literary work can contain a moral precept that is supposed to be valid for mankind as a whole. It seems to be part and parcel of our cultural tradition to formulate interpretative verdicts in moral terms.[6]

Students are not equally good readers, for which reason the teacher should not be ashamed of beginning the analytical work on a fairly elementary level. Many students will find it inspiring and rewarding to move in the direction of what they take to be an expansion of their experience; man seems to have an innate need of learning more. A teacher will often be able to sense the enjoyment of his students when they move from the narrative to the interpretative level.

On the other hand it is a fact that, to some students, interpretation is reminiscent of a kind of dressage that they are highly skeptical of. You need only consult the genre called memoirs to realize that a good many outstanding writers and authors have had their personal enjoyment of literature more or less permanently destroyed owing to interpretations that were little more than inane grinding.

Interpretative systems

Many interpretative systems and models are beset with a pedagogic weakness in that they tend to be too simple or too complicated. The simple ones are a series of commonplaces couched in heavy and pretentious Greco-Latin terminology. They invariably reveal their insufficiency with texts of some complexity, and they are too all-embracing to be applicable to the peculiarities of individual works. And it is often peculiarities that present an interpretative challenge.

The complicated ones are so abstract as to be unmanageable, and they may degenerate into separate descriptions for individual works. And yet they, too, are deficient where the profoundest secrets of a work are concerned. Systems are comparable to templates, and a decent work of art refuses to be squeezed into a ready-made mould. The students may learn some impressive-sounding foreign words, but it is highly questionable whether they really benefit from such a superstructure, be it ever so ambitious.

However, the alternative to schematic formalism need not be fluttering chaos. With practically all groups of recipients, it is possible to achieve a certain level of method. Good pedagogy is very rarely devoid of method for the simple reason that students find it difficult to grasp what is unstructured and diffuse. It is certainly possible to teach students more than a modicum of method, or perhaps it would be more correct to say methodical approach, which will prevent them from flying off at too many tangents. Experience shows that the most rewarding procedure is a combination of something 'from within' and something 'from without', i.e. some systematism of progression in the descriptive stage plus, in the more advanced stages, some exploitation of pedagogically relevant factors in the existing models. Such 'cross-fertilization' or didactic pluralism presupposes that the teacher is familiar with a bunch of critical theories so as to be able to exploit their pedagogic potential. Pluralism implies that no single model can answer all questions. However, pluralism is not incompatible with a systematic approach. Nor is it synonymous with that type of intellectual laziness that rates all opinions and suggestions equally highly. Superficially, pluralism may seem to sacrifice some of the cogency that we normally associate with scholarly investigation. On the other hand, it does not brand deviation as heresy, and its broad-mindedness will permit it to include even conflicting conceptions of the same work.

Most models will explain many things, but every model has its limitations. If you stick fanatically to one model, you exclude the use, and the usefulness, of many others. Thus, the 'butterfly' approach suggested by the French-Lithuanian critic Algirdas Greimas is certainly useful when dealing with narrative literature of the folk-tale type. If dressed in flesh and blood, Greimas' concepts (helper, receiver, enemy, etc.) may contribute to some clarification, also because his 'agents' are archetypes. But it cannot account satisfactorily for the subtler nuances to be found is novels, and its usefulness is next to non-existent where lyrical poetry is concerned. If all texts are put on a Procrustes' bed, spontaneous glimpses of insight may be ignored, but the tentative and experimental suggestions that are a *sine qua non* of the teaching of literature are not going to be synonymous with the teacher's pontificating.

According to Michel Foucault, every age has some basic paradigms ('cadres de pensée) that determine what questions and answers are legitimate and justifiable. The texts of a given age are reflections of such paradigms, or models that show how things work.[7] The German critic Edmund Husserl has put forward some analogous theories: there is a system of expectations and probabilities surrounding a given text. That system, which morphs from one age to another, is called by Husserl 'horizons'. The 'horizon', then, becomes the context – in the broadest sense of the word – that a given age permits a text to illustrate and exemplify.[8] Both Foucault and Husserl seem to have been inspired by Theodore Kuhn's theory of paradigms,[9] which was, originally, thought not to be applicable to literary criticism.

The history of literary criticism demonstrates that, even if they are both social scientists and not literary professionals, Foucault and Husserl have got a valid point. To give one instance, the 18th century found value in works that by and large conformed to the reader's expectations: imitation of classical authors was the recognized and respected procedure, and a considerable part of the aesthetic experience consisted in the pleasure of recognition. Our age looks differently at that issue: what confers value on a text may often be the fact that there is a gap between its contents and the reader's expectations. So, our 'cadre de pensée' differs from that of the 18th century.

Besides, it is an empirical fact that some models are more palatable to students than others. At first sight, one form of pedagogic treatment would seem to be fairly obvious, viz. the progression that consists in making beginners start from scratch and 'move upwards'. As was mentioned earlier, that is not the only way of apprehending new material, which is proved by the way children learn to speak their mother tongue. Secondly, all experience goes to show that students do not mind 'standing on tiptoe', i.e. tackling a seemingly hopelessly knotty text if they are somehow captured by either the language or the content. Still, the fact remains that a story by e.g. Graham Greene is more 'reader-friendly' than a poem by Yeats.

E.D. Hirsch Jr. is convinced that there are universally valid interpretations.[10] His argument is that if it is not possible to determine meanings unequivocally, the concept of knowledge itself is at stake. According to Hirsch, the study of what a text means has so far too often been synonymous with what it means to a particular critic: the interpreter has decided, more or less arbitrarily, what points in the text he wants to concentrate on, which means that the interpretation is not carried on by the inherent nature of the text (whatever that may mean!).

Hirsch shifts the emphasis to the author. The point is to find what the author intended to say, for what other criterion of validity can be imagined? Again, an obvious objection by a critic of Hirsch would say that his theory is empirically unfounded and therefore only seemingly convincing. For one thing, it is possible to draw conclusions as to the author's intention only via a process of interpretation – and even then, much of it remains guesswork, an Unknown replaced by another Unknown.

Secondly – and paradoxically – Hirsch admits that the author does not always know himself what he means, which of course complicates matters considerably for the critic. Thirdly, even in cases where the author has stated his intention or intentions explicitly, what he has expressed in his work may very well differ from his avowed intention (D.H. Lawrence said, "Don't trust the writer, trust the tale!'), which does not necessarily make his work a failure. To get out of this dilemma, Hirsch suggests that competent critics must attempt to reach an agreement about the author's intention. He seems to be unaware that this solution places the ultimate responsibility for the author's intention at the critics' door.

A theory like Hirsch's is extremely unwieldy from a pedagogic point of view. Extensive reading of an author's oeuvre or of the writings of a period is required if one is to state with a reasonable amount of probability what an author's intention *really* was. By the way, who is going to select the 'competent critics'?

It is not difficult to find texts that allow alternative interpretations. Even if conflicting, they may be equally plausible, or at least possible. The little boy in Hans Christian Andersen's fairy tale *The Emperor's New Clothes* sees through deceit and dissimulation. He alone calls attention to the fact that the emperor has no clothes on, thus showing that in his childish innocence he refuses to be imposed on by the splendour that takes in the adults. That is what one interpreter would take to be the message of the tale. But to another interpreter, the little boy may be an officious spoilsport whose lack of imagination ruins a game that the participants enjoyed playing for a short while, perfectly aware that they were being momentarily hoodwinked. Both interpretations, though mutually exclusive, are legitimate, but which of them is the better one, and what do they tell us about Andersen's intentions?

Today, many critics consider it an asset for a literary work to be susceptible of several, equally justified interpretations; on the other hand, everybody recognizes the greatness of Dante's *Divine Comedy*, which admits of little latitude of interpretation. Incidentally, it would be interesting to investigate why some periods prefer works with limited interpretative possibilities – thus, much 17th century literature has the implicit or explicit aim to 'justify the ways of God to man' – whereas other ages encourage expansive readings, indeed look upon it as a liability that the possibilities of exegesis are limited.

In spite of the existence of different, admissible 'frames of thinking' determined by the Zeitgeist of different ages, the fact remains that interpretations are individual achievements. The interpreter's own biography, in the widest sense of the word, the sum of his education, experiences, memories, etc. play a decisive part. The goal of the interpretation is shaped partly by the text, partly by the choices made by the reader.

The Satisfactory Interpretation

An interpretation worth its name should be *adequate, coherent*, and *plausible*. Adequate, or suitable, in that an interpreter must not go against the grain of the text; a scientific essay should not be treated as a fairy tale for children. It should be coherent, or 'hang together', in that it must establish correspondences between the various components of the text. Not all ingredients are serviceable, and there will always be distracting factors. But, ideally speaking, the interpretation must establish a distinction between relevant and irrelevant and must not end up as a series of isolated observations. It should be plausible, or reasonable, in that the text is not to be boiled down to a handful of sociological facts, or be made a key to the author's intellectual make-up.

An interpretation should give its readers a sense that we are capable of arranging and illustrating the multifarious facets of existence in such a way that we are not pushed over by them. It is a question of making cosmos out of chaos, of establishing stability in the midst of something that at first sight appears as confusion, of acquiring a feeling that our experience can be structured, a feeling that we are stronger than the disorder that tends to arise when things are left to themselves.

There is something inherently self-confirming about successful interpretations, and the result is often accompanied by a feeling of conviction and reassurance. Much of the evidence we use to substantiate our hypothesis is some that we chose when we formulated the hypothesis. That is the reason why an interpretation comes to seem 'inevitable', for a possible change of angle of approach would imply that some of the ingredients of the text must assume a different character and function. As Stanley Fish points out,[11] a person who analyses a text according to a certain model is likely to select such items in the text as the model is capable of recognizing and handling. If one of the categories of the model is syntactic ambiguity, one of the questions prompted by the analysis will naturally be: 'Does this text show any instance of syntactic ambiguity?' Thus there is a danger that the analysis will create the work, or parts of it, rather than be loyal to it. The viability or vulnerability of a given model can be demonstrated by bringing its criteria to bear in different texts. And the question might be discussed whether there are some basic features that are common to models, and if so, what are they?

The satisfactory interpretation is not necessarily the one that includes the greatest number of points: success is not obtained by a simple addition of what the reader regards as the relevant indicators of a text. An interpretation should be capable of specifying possible implications, and the implications must be combined with, or susceptible of combination with, external facts of a historical, biographical, social, economic, etc. kind.

Since interpretation of literary texts does not have the same degree of objectivity as the results of science, it seems plausible to talk about the 'correctness of intersubjectivity', i.e. a well-established consensus among several qualified critics' readings of the same texts. The individual interpretation of a work is descriptive, but once it has been 'intersubjectively' approved, it acquires the status of something normative in that future critics will have to make up their minds about it, perhaps even be guided by some of its suggestions. Admittedly, the concept of 'a competent critic' is a vague designation.

However, since students are not professional critics, teaching should inspire an imaginative and bold approach to textual work. Random shots may prove fertile, and in any case they are preferable to silence on the part of the participants, especially if they feel that silence has been imposed on them by the teacher's more or less pronounced skepticism towards their suggestions.

Against Interpretation

Experience shows that the alternative to a teacher-inspired, or even teacher-guided, interpretation is – no interpretation. That is of course not the end of the world, but the question has been raised, also by serious writers, whether literary interpretations are useful or necessary at all. Prominent among the spokespersons for leaving the text, and art in general, alone, is Susan Sontag, who in her essay *Against Interpretation*[12] takes a radical anti-interpretation view: a text does not *mean*, it *is*. That is also what Archibald MacLeish said in his poem *Ars Poetica*, of which the finishing lines are: "A poem should not mean/but be". Art is not *about* something, Sontag goes on to say, it *is* something, a thing *in* the world, not a comment *on* the world. Even the simplest feeling is indescribable in its totality, and a work of art is a working up of something that does not admit of verbal formulation. The work of art is the message which the artist gives to the world, and it is irrelevant to attempt to split it up in form and content. To Susan Sontag, the essential value is *transparency*, i.e. the fact that the thing itself appears with luminous clarity. Accordingly, it is a sign of inferior quality if a work of art can be understood in more ways than one: such cases are evidence of a deplorable redundancy. It is not made clear what kind of redundancy is referred to, or who is to be held responsible.

Sontag and her allies may have a point here: reviewers of music and the pictorial arts sometimes couch their articles in a cryptic language that is anything but transparent or even comprehensible, and behind it all is the problem of formulating the achievements of one branch of art in the medium of another, i.e. language. We may refer to the centuries-old discussion of the *ut pictura poesis* tradition.[13] Paradoxically, Sontag's ideal, transparency remains pretty opaque. Has Shakespeare got more transparency, also formally speaking, than a story in a weekly magazine? Her postulate borders on a tautology: great art is characterized by transparency, she says, which is the specific type of lucidity found in – great art.

From a pedagogic point of view, theories like Sontag's are unmanageable. She gives no guidelines as to how a critic can be able to show how the work of art 'is' as it is. She concedes that works of art can be described, and the literary ones also paraphrased, but gives no details, and she repeatedly insists on the significance of concentrating on the form. However, she does not tell us which formal aspects are preferable to others, and she does not indicate possible ways of cultivating the reader's or the critic's appreciation of the form. She evades a discussion of concepts like correctness of compatibility where different readers' approaches are concerned, and seems to exclude the possibility that understanding of the content may be a source of enrichment, indeed a necessary first step towards aesthetic enjoyment. And it does not occur to her that the individual reader's understanding and enjoyment might be enhanced if explicated and discussed.

It seems that Sontag leads readers and critics up a blind alley, and a teacher is at a loss with her postulates. However, the opposite procedure of what she suggests, viz. draining the text dry, rigidly and unimaginatively, making sure that every detail is put in its appropriate pigeonhole, is equally hopeless. So, once more, the teacher has to find his own way between the cave of Scylla and the whirlpool of Charybdis. Excessive leaning on models of textual treatment may degenerate into fatuous pigeon-holing. A chosen angle of approach must be flexible enough to allow, perhaps even encourage, deviations from the beaten track. Pedantry is deadening, and different genres require different analysis techniques. But then again, the teacher's principal occupation is not to devise new and 'smashing' approaches for each individual text. A teacher's techniques must not be suspended in mid-air: chaos is counterproductive.

Paradigms, then, are useful conventions, but they are not unchangeable fossils, and it is definitely possible to pour new wine into old bottles. And the alternative to schematic formalism does not have to be confused chaos. The teacher should of course call his students' attention to the fact that paradigms change and that they are, ultimately, children of their age. And he should freely acknowledge that his own interpretation, however brilliant, does not and cannot lay claim to universal and everlasting validity. For interpretations are individual achievements. Every interpretation begins as a tentative guess – some of them end as one, too! The quality of the guess depends on factors like the interpreter's knowledge, experience, intuition, and ingenuity, and some guesses are 'better' than others though, sadly enough, nobody has as yet devised a method of informed guessing. The interpretation process will be characterized by leaps of the imagination and bold hypothesis-making. What is known is gradually integrated into something unknown, familiar phenomena appear in a fresh light, and connecting links present themselves.

An interpretation is a probability judgement. It can be rejected by fresh insights, which does not necessarily mean that the first one was null and void. There are few, if any, procedures that are at the same time of general validity and applicable to a specific situation.

The fact that interpretation is determined by conventions and paradigms plus contributions provided by the interpreter have some pedagogic consequences. It is obviously uphill work to familiarize today's students with the interpretative conventions of earlier ages to such a degree that the pleasure they get out of reading a text by, say, Pope, will be commensurable with that of one of Pope's contemporaries. However, the point is that the delight that a 21st century student derives from a work that is 300 years old need not be inferior to that of an intelligent contemporary even though the modern reader's criteria are different: the difference is one of kind, but not necessarily of degree.

There is probably a good deal of truth in the well-known dictum that a valuable book is one that has been able to 'survive' one or more shifts of paradigm. What that means is that worthwhile texts are such as have stood the test of time, and there is a considerable number of works that can be profitably analysed according to our paradigms even if they are not identical with those of a contemporary. An analysis of

Hamlet along Freudian lines has yielded valuable new insight into the character of the Prince of Denmark. By the same token, the Polish director Ian Kott fluttered the critical dovecotes in the 1960s with his reflections on, and performances of, Shakespeare's dramas in a style that was profoundly influenced by the political thinking of that decade.

It is conceivable – and perfectly legitimate – that, in his choice of material, the teacher may *also* be guided by pedagogical considerations besides the 'quality' ones. Thus he might ask himself what forms of work a given text may inspire, and how far he can count on his students' active participation. The students' ages and the character of the text determine the extent to which the cooperation becomes less asymmetrical, i.e. the mental gap between the two sides of the desk is reduced.

When to Stop

One of the noblest purposes of the teaching of literature ought to be to inspire students not to abandon the reading and enjoyment of literature when they are not taught it in school any more. So there is a good deal to be said in favour of initiating the students into some procedures, not full-fledged models, but tools that are not too complicated and which are not, on the other hand, so simplified as to take them nowhere, tools that help them to see what it might be profitable to look for in a text, and what to do with what they find. And, of course, reservations against universal models should not make the teacher shy away from theorizing as such.

Literature is something that has to be understood *and* enjoyed, *prodesse et delectare.* Both ingredients are significant. Experience shows that the better the understanding is, the richer the experience will be. Accordingly, no teacher will be content if his students' experience becomes comparable to indeterminable porridge. And it should not be forgotten that admiration based on reason and understanding will do no harm to the delicate flower of literature.

But when does a teacher tell himself that enough is enough? Ernst Gombrich, the Anglo-Austrian critic of art, discusses the issue in the form of a parallel with the creative artist's situation: the latter 'knows', i.e. has an intuitive feeling that the artefact he has made is 'right'.[14] Textual work would seem to provide a parallel. Work should stop when the teacher, and hopefully also the students, feel that a meaningful unity has been reached. That is not tantamount to saying that the text should be squeezed to the last drop, but that it should be feasible so incorporate, say, 75 per cent of the items of the text into the final result. Of course the experienced teacher will know that not *any* 75 per cent will do. A result that is felt to be 'right' will usually admit of few loose ends. On the other hand, in some cases the very point may be that there are insoluble elements of obscurity, as is seen in Gerald Manley Hopkins' poetry.

So, a good policy is to stop before dissection becomes murder.

CHAPTER EIGHT

The Pedagogical Challenges of the Different Genres

Genre

The affiliation of literary texts to different genres (particular types of writing that share certain features) is a centuries-old tradition: we have preserved examples of tragedy, comedy, and epics (the forerunners of the modern novel) from ancient Greece and Rome. Those three genres still cover the majority of fictional works written today. An interesting pedagogic experiment can be to analyse the extent to which the preponderance of a given genre coincides with and is determined by the contemporary cultural climate. The Elizabethan age favoured drama, early 19th century sees a lot of 'personal' poetry, the later 19th century is dominated by the long novel.

Attitudes to the concept of genre also vary through the centuries: 17th century authors saw tragedy (and 'heroic' painting) as the apex of a hierarchy, which was never properly filled; indeed, sometimes they seem to be more preoccupied with the genre affiliation of a work than with the substance of it. To them, genre had become a prescriptive term, i.e. it laid down a set of rules that a work must obey in order to be in accordance with the requirements of good taste (la bienséance). Even if the emphasis was on content more than form, a work was not so much judged by what would today be called its inherent qualities as the extent to which it satisfied the peculiarities of its genre. That knowledge is a *sine qua non* if modern students are to do justice to some of Dryden's tragedies.

The modern attitude to genres (as to so many other authorities) is considerably less deferential: genres are rather recognized as practical categories, and experience shows that successful works are often positioned in the borderland between two genres: the Western is indebted to the short story as well as to the pastoral; the musical harks back to opera, but also to comedy and tragedy. By the same token, today we accept mixed genres, which were anathema to e.g. the Neo-Classicists: 21st century criticism has no theoretical objections to tragi-comedy.

The well-known series of verbal tools that are at the disposal of an author of literary works (composition, rhyme, etc.) is not equally distributed among the genres: thus, there are few rhymes in a novel. In the following pages, the pedagogic potentialities of the different 'kinds', as the Neo-Classicists termed the genres, will be investigated. The ordering principle is frequency of occurrence in a given genre: 'composition' is placed under the Novel because it is one of the supporting pillars of that genre. The intention is not to signify that a ten-line poem is devoid of composition. In other cases, the criterion is one of manageability: 'style' is treated under Poetry because it becomes unwieldy and often inconclusive in the case of a 300-page novel.

A teacher of literature will be able to exploit and elaborate on the almost instinctive sense of genre affiliation which his students possess. Sometimes the title of the text may be helpful, but even beginners will know that a text which is almost exclusively made up of characters speaking to each other belongs under the heading of Drama. What this means is that, even if the technical term may not be known, the characteristics of the genres are familiar to virtually all readers of literature.

Genre transposition is an attractive work form: students are asked, singly or in groups, to write a text in a different genre from that in which it exists. Obvious transitions are from short story to drama, and vice versa. But poems, too, can be written as narratives, in fact, when we paraphrase a poem, we transpose poetry to prose. Such 'transfers' provide good insight into the characteristics of the genres, their possibilities and restrictions. If, for example, students are asked to dramatize a short story, they will have to make up their minds on the following questions: how is the background information of the story to be conveyed, in the shape of speeches or as a stage direction? How is the protagonist's thinking activity to be illustrated on the stage? How can a human being's character be made reasonably comprehensible when there is no narrator to brief the spectator, etc?

That is not an easy task. But in their attempt to cope with it, students will receive some hints as to why, for instance, the author chose the form of the essay, and not of a poem. No less importantly, it will give them some respect for the craftsmanship of the artefact.

Poetry

A major pedagogic challenge when dealing with poetry is not so much to attempt a definition of the genre, but rather to rectify some misconceptions shared also by some students of literature. In their perception, poetry 'is to do with feelings' and deals with a restricted spectrum of subjects; it makes use of a rhymed language that is entirely different from 'everyday language'. There is some truth in those statements, but one of the tasks of literary pedagogy is to test the validity of such generalizations.

In actual fact, poetry is capable of depicting a huge number of the facets of life, indeed in principle there are no limits to what it is possible to write poems about. Admittedly, few poems have been written about a middle-aged woman hurrying to the supermarket in her slippers just before closing time. However, Lloyd Evans wrote *An Ode to Joy-Riding*, and the first stanza of a poem by William Carlos Williams (*This is Just to say)* runs as follows: "I have eaten the plums which were in the icebox/And which you were probably saving for breakfast./Forgive me, they were delicious,/So sweet and so cold." And if rhymes are claimed as the ultimate criterion of 'poetry', much of Browning's oeuvre will have to be excommunicated.

Poetry does deal with feelings (in any case a vague designation), but so do other genres, e.g. Shakespeare's dramas and Dickens' novels. The prompting of emotional reactions is not the exclusive property of poems. But when we read a love poem, we may have an experience that, in its intensity, is similar to the narrator's own. It is perhaps because we sense the direct appeal so clearly – many love poems are fairly short – that feelings have come to be regarded as the peculiar province of poetry.

Poetry is often remarkably context-free; historical or biographical information may have to be added. Poetry aims at a greater precision than a long narrative. The selection that has taken place in e.g. a love poem is worth studying, not only because it differs from that made in a novel, but also in its own right. Who are the 'you' or 'my love' referred to in a love poem? In poems, we frequently read about somebody who calls himself

'I', but who is not necessarily the narrator, addressing a 'you', who is not me, the reader, and talking about things that are, strictly speaking, none of my business. So here is more than meets the eye, which necessitates deeper digging. It is obvious that the speaker wants to get in contact with us. If he has not, in our opinion, made his point crystal clear, that may spur us to on to try to find out what he 'really' wants. The structuralists may lend a hand to the teacher on this point: as they see it, a poem is a network of relationships, not assembled like clockwork toys, but built up organically like a plant.

Poetry is more evidently conscious of form than prose (even if it is possible to talk about prose rhythm). What makes poetry seem concentrated, sometimes even condensed, is the fact that, especially in shorter poems, virtually all the words are the fruit of careful deliberation. The poet is a craftsman, a creator, who does his best to lick his material into shape.

It is true that a poem may be felt to be inconsistent with conventional ideas of the patterns of coherent thinking. But so do fairy tales, space dramas and utopias. Besides, virtually all literature invites man to be an *animal rationale* as well as an *animal emotionale.* Dr. Johnson gave his didactic message in *Rasselas* in the shape of a poem. One of the teacher's tasks is to demonstrate to the students that poetry is not an irresponsible letting loose of vague or 'great' feelings, but that, on the contrary, poetry disciplines feelings owing to its extremely precise use of the language.

Style

If four people are asked to describe the same event or sequence of events in their own words, it can be predicted with a reasonable amount of certainty that their accounts will not be identical. Not only will they make idiosyncratic selections of the material and have different priorities. There are also bound to be differences in their vocabulary and syntax, depending on their ages, social affiliations, attitudes to the story, purpose in telling it, etc. You can say that each of the narrators has his own style.

Each of the four descriptions will contain more information than is immediately given by the linguistic structures. In any text there is an overall organizing principle influencing the formulation of the message. That principle is the form or style of the message.

In all the arts, analysis of the style of the finished product is an integral part of the aesthetic evaluation of it, so a teacher of literature must devote a considerable amount of attention to it. However, style is not easy to define, even though the discipline called stylistics emerged as a reaction against what was felt to be vague and subjective within literary criticism.

For teaching purposes, it has proved practical to centre questions of style on three main points, viz. *choice of words*, *form of words*, and *concatenation of words*.

The choice of words, or *vocabulary*, includes e.g. the question of word class domination: what character does the presence of many adjectives and few verbs confer on this text? or the verbs might be analysed, not only in terms of tense and mood, but also of 'kind': are they descriptive or empty of content (as is the case with the verb be (the *copula*) and its synonyms)? Are the nouns mainly abstract or concrete ones, etc.?

A sure winner where vocabulary is concerned is *the substitution test*: for the four-legged draught animal 'horse', English has several variants, e.g. jade, hack, steed, nag, mount, and pony (donkey is less relevant here!). What happens to a given passage if for *jade* we substitute *steed*? Why has the narrator chosen *jade* for this particular context?

Features to be analysed under the heading of word form are e.g. the use made of slang or archaisms or Latinisms, the form of pronouns, or the relative weight given to the active and the passive form of verbs. James Macpherson's *Ossian* poems (1760–63) were a forgery. What linguistic devices did he avail himself of in order to convince his readers that the poems had been written by a legendary Scottish bard?

The concatenation of words, or *syntax*, deals with word order and the length of sentences, and with the distribution of parataxis (coordination) and hypotaxis (subordination); it is a well-known fact that many texts have several 'layers' of hypotaxis, one sentence being subordinated to another, which is, in its turn, subordinated, etc. The use of periphrasis (or circumlocution) comes in here, as in Pope's 'finny tribe' for 'fish, i.e. an adjective plus a generic term. Dickens' presentation of the participants of the court scene in *The Pickwick Papers,* more particularly Serjeant Buzfuz's speech for the prosecution, offers abundant illustrations of hypotaxis. Passages of that display of oratorical fireworks have proved very suitable for stage performances as well as recitation purposes.

It is true that we find in poetry many words that are used in non-poetical texts as well: forest, sunshine, lake, etc. Every linguistic feature is potentially of stylistic interest. In poetry, words are selected because they convey more than 'mere meaning', and the word itself is part of what the poet wants to say. Poetry often deals, in concentration, with fundamental issues in human life, such as death, love, nature, and such concepts and the many abstractions that poetry contains, require a certain vocabulary.

Longinus was satisfied that there is such a thing as 'beautiful words' which are "in deed and in fact the very light of the spirit". The Romanticists were very fond of the word 'bower'. That is an interesting discussion point: are there such things as 'beautiful words' today? If so, name some of them. On the other hand, it is questionable that there exists a type of language that is an objective and value-free medium of human communication.

Most 18th century poets were convinced that poetry needs a specific language. Their *poetic diction* is worth some consideration, not only for its use of periphrasis (Pope's 'the ethereal plain' for 'the heavens'), but also for its dependence on contemporary ideas of taste and decorum, which held that only certain words and grammatical arrangements are appropriate for poetry.

Dr. Johnson maintained that the language of poetry was "refined from the grossness of domestic use", a statement that relegated 'everyday language' to an inferior position. The shift of paradigm that was inaugurated with the advent of Romanticism is another proof of the intimate relationship between content and form: Wordsworth's subjects differed from Pope's, and the change necessitated a different kind of language.

In the Preface to the *Lyrical Ballads*, 2nd ed., 1800, Wordsworth focusses on what he calls "vicious poetic diction": "there neither is, nor can be, any essential difference between the language of prose and metrical composition" – a postulate that would relegate most of the poetry written before the 1790s. Students should be asked to investigate to what extent he followed his own precepts, e.g. by comparing *Lucy Gray* with the *Intimations of Immortality*.

The language used in modern poetry shows so many varieties that it will be next to impossible to lay down the law for poetic diction. What features, for example, are shared by Gerald Manley Hopkins and Robert Frost? By Sylvia Plath and Philip Larkin? Few, apart from the fact that they wrote poems. Accordingly, poetic diction is a phenomenon of mainly historical interest.

Stanley Fish says that when we look upon a text as being literary, it is because we have decided to pay particular attention to resources that are always contained in the language.[1] There is an element of truth in the statement, for some texts are composed in such a way that they immediately invite 'literary' reading. However, it is a very broad generalization, for we will certainly also pay attention to the wording of an insurance policy.

Kenneth Burke has made a very apposite comment on the difference between semantic meaning, i.e. what appears in the everyday use of the language, and poetic meaning:[2] the semantic meaning is comparable to the address of a letter, viz. the name (sc. of a person), the street, the postal code, the town, and the country. But, as he says, "when you have isolated the individual by the proper utilizing of the postal process, you have not at all adequately encompassed his 'meaning'. He means one thing to his family, another to his boss, another to his underlings, another to his creditors, etc."[3] All those 'identifications' are analogous to poetic meaning, which is more than 'mere' semantic meaning. To put it differently: the semantic approach stresses the role of the observer, the poetic approach that of the participant. Owing to its transparency, the theory ought to gain favour with teachers of literature.

The French critic Michel Riffaterre underlines the role of style as a factor in the communication process: style is the sum total of items used to induce the receiver to relate to the sender's message.[4] Style is the element that shows the impact on the act of communication, and the sender may want to make his message vague or succinct, lucid or obscure. The postulate is a suitable discussion starter.

Style is a product of specific ways of making things. Style is the result of human activities, for a stone is not said to have style. An author's style is his way of handling language; he conveys something about his artistic perception and practice, perhaps also about his psychology.

Pointing to this or that stylistic feature in isolation is, as a rule, of very limited interest to students. Nobody understands more of a poem because he recognizes the rhyme scheme of it. Experience shows that style is an unwieldy phenomenon for students to handle. Therefore, questions concerning style should be precise and limited to one aspect, e.g. How does the narrator's use of Latinisms influence the text?

Denotation and Connotation

Roughly speaking, denotation equals dictionary meaning. Connotation is the supplementary value that is added to the purely referential function of a word. It is a culture-determined aura of associations evoked by a word, and it is characteristic that we usually talk about connotations in the plural. Connotations cannot be found in a dictionary, for they are the shades of meaning surrounding the dictionary meaning, and at the same time they are an integral part of the meaning which the word has to a native speaker.

A good key to clarify the difference between the two is to look at the chemical formula H_2O and its everyday verbal equivalent, water. The chemical formula has informative value and no more, whereas the word 'water' evokes a multitude of associations, indeed it is questionable whether anyone can hear the word 'water' without getting, at the same time, some associations connected with the liquid.

Connotations may be individual, e.g. Proust's well-known Madeleine cake or Greene's baize door, or embedded in a cultural custom. To a person brought up in the Christian tradition, the word 'crucifixion' will evoke ideas of Christ's death on the cross rather than the conventional Roman method of punishment. And 'democracy', perhaps the most misused of words, will be lost in a tangle of political and philosophical associations.

Metaphor and Simile

"But at my back I always hear/ Time's winged chariot hurrying near/ And yonder all before us lie/ Deserts of vast eternity," says Marvel in his poem *To His Coy Mistress*. The gist of the lines is that time is running short, and that after death it will be the Great Nothing. To give us an impression of the passing of time, the poet furnishes the personification 'time' with a chariot which has wings – one of the swiftest means of transportation imaginable at the time when the poem was written. The word 'desert' usually evokes images of vast expanses of sand or barren land. Here, the meaning has been 'carried over' to the concept of eternity. That identification makes the poet's experience more precise to himself, as well as to his readers, at the same time inducing or forcing the readers to look upon things the way he does. Our conception of 'the way things are' will be enlarged if we admit the justification of the synthesis he has made, even though he postulates an identification between two spheres of experience that we would, in 'normal' circumstances, consider widely different.

Metaphor literally means 'carrying over', and transfers of Marvel's kind are the basic elements of literature. The 'illogical' juxtaposition that is its distinctive mark is pedagogically valuable on account of the newly-aroused associations. The metaphoric use adds precision to the description. However, it is noteworthy that it is not the precision of science. The metaphor throws light on some areas of existence that are difficult of access by drawing parallels with areas that are more familiar: abstractions are made more palpable when measured by the standards of the physical world. Consequently, the use of metaphors is particularly widespread in cases where ordinary language has difficulty in finding a covering designation. Thus, there are few things that can be said about God that are not metaphorical, and how does one describe eternity? The American writer Normal Mailer once said that if the universe is a lock, the key to open it must be a metaphor. The metaphor exploits the potentialities of language to the full and thus enhances our comprehension of the world we live in.

Dissolving a metaphor and a simile in their constituent parts is not just pedantic pigeon-holing. From a pedagogic point of view, it can be highly rewarding to get closer to the creative process, to begin to have an inkling of how a poetic image – one of the noblest tools of literature – comes into existence. Students may get a thrill analogous to that of a biologist engaged in genetic engineering.

I. A. Richards has suggested a model for dissolving a metaphor which has proved pedagogically workable. In a sentence like Anne Ridler's 'Lovers whose lifted hands are like candles in winter', Richards distinguishes three ingredients: (1) the subject, that which is talked about (lovers' hands); that is called the *tenor*. (2) the predicate, or explanation or definition (candles in winter); that is called the *vehicle*, because it is the means of transport. (3) the area which must be necessarily shared by tenor and vehicle for the metaphor to be comprehensible; that is called the *ground*. The common area here is that lovers' hands are warm in a cold world, just as candles give warmth in cold weather.

Some points should be emphasized in connection with metaphors: for an 'over-carrying' to be successful, tenor and vehicle, when united, must give a deeper and more varied meaning than either of them would have in isolation. Moreover, in order to appreciate the metaphor, the reader must be familiar with the denotations as well as the connotations of tenor and vehicle. In the metaphor with the lovers' lifted hands, the metaphor loses its impact if, for example, the reader lives in a climate that does not know cold winters. 'Candles in winter' are the words that break a purely informative concatenation of words, so that is where the metaphoric element is found. However, it is a specific aspect of 'candles' that is operative here, viz. their capacity to give warmth, not their shape or colour.

It will be seen that quite a number of words are needed to paraphrase a metaphor. That is one reason why the shortcuts of metaphors occur so frequently in poetry, which has often got a limited amount of space at its disposal, and which often displays what might be called a concentration of language. As Aristotle pointed out, "the greatest (sc. excellence) of all is to be happy in the use of metaphor, for it is this alone which cannot be acquired, and which, consisting in a quick discernment of resemblances, is a certain mark of genius."[5] Talking about a thing as if it were something else is probably the most effective way of catching a reader's attention.

When the students have dissolved the metaphor, possible next steps might be to examine whether a text has got many or only a few metaphors and whether they form a pattern, and to discuss the degree to which their presence and their kind colour the text.

Simile

Metaphor underlines the *identification.* In the sentence 'his face was a sheet', an intellectual effort, or a 'leap' is required on the reader's part. A simile stresses the *comparison* and is, more often than not, just a metaphor with an added 'as' or 'like': 'his face was like a sheet'. For some metaphors, then, it is possible to construct a corresponding simile by supplying the vehicle with 'as or 'like'; but to make matters perfectly clear, some supplementary words will frequently be required: in a sentence like 'he was like an elephant', is the ground bulk, heaviness, slowness of movement, thickness of hide, or long memory? Only the context will show. The context will also show which of the aspects of a metaphor are relevant in a given situation: when we say that Peter is a rat, we do not mean that he has a long tail. But, curiously, in the case of a metaphor, little supplementary information is necessary. The relevant 'carrying over' is grasped intuitively.

Symbol

In symbols, we see an extension of meaning from a literal sense to a figurative one; when 'flame' is used in the sense of 'passion', we say that flame is a symbol of, or symbolizes, passion. It is important not to overlook the fact that the literal meaning of a word is still perceptible in the symbolic use of it: flame denotes fire, and symbolizes passion. As is the case with metaphor, a symbol achieves its effect by the tension that is established between the two meanings.

This figure :† represents two lines (or sticks of wood, or pieces of stone), and between them they make up what we call a cross. To those who are brought up in the Christian tradition, the association to the crucifixion of Christ is obvious. That means that the figure evokes thoughts of death and redemption. Thus two lines come to symbolize one of the greatest events within the Christian tradition. The primary meaning of a symbol is a physical one, and it refers to a spiritual or psychological phenomenon. But the point is that the transition happens, and can only be grasped, via the physical word.

Like metaphors, symbols select specific aspects and ignore others: when the dove comes to symbolize peace, it is to do with its quiet brooding and presumed lack of aggressiveness towards other birds. Actually, the language has a designation for the same bird with little or no symbolic value, viz. pigeon. The latter's appropriateness as a symbol is dubious, not least because it is known to be a carrier of dangerous infectious diseases.

Symbols are conventional within a given cultural group. The cross has decidedly negative symbol value in the Muslim world. Many symbols seem to be as old as civilization itself, e.g. the use of a skull to symbolize death. And some 'transitions' are so common as to be almost predictable: from member to class (oak symbolizing strong, sturdy, and robust objects); from one kingdom to another (oak symbolizing a strong personality); from concrete to abstract (oak symbolizing toughness, stubbornness, etc.). Several philosophers and anthropologists incline to the belief that man is by nature a symbol-creating being, besides being a rational and an emotional being. In the case of the cross, the act of symbolization proceeded by fairly logical steps – the starting-point was a familiar Roman type of punishment. But the transition may sometimes be completely arbitrary: why should a triangle stood on its head that is placed at the end of a stick mean 'major road ahead'? But once it has been fixed, the symbolic value usually persists. However, 'red' is not unambiguous: it may represent danger, but also the life-giving blood. In a traffic context it never means 'go'.

The really tricky symbols are the individual ones that are idiosyncratic to one or only a few users. A case in point is Yeats' use of Byzantium. Some of them seem made for the nonce, and will require some biographical background information. With advanced students, it will be rewarding to investigate the symbolic designations that succeeding generations have attributed to various 'great' abstract concepts like power, victory, being tested and passing or failing the test, adulthood, sexuality. That will show them that symbolization is not only abstraction, but also enrichment because, like other items of imagery, it is an extension of meaning. It will also increase their awareness of the cultural background of Western civilization and, ultimately, provide a discreet approach towards comprehending more of the concept of meaning.

Rhyme and Metre

Rhyme and metre give coherence to a poem and significant information to the reader in that they are a sort of frame separating the linguistic garb of the poem from everyday use of the language. But they are not pedagogically fascinating, and it is a waste of time to learn multifarious stanzaic patterns and rhyme schemes by heart because they add little to the value of the text. The fact that there are different sonnet structures is of limited pedagogical interest. However, it may be a sobering experience for students to try to write a sonnet of their own. It may instill some respect in them for the competence of the sonnet writers, no matter what pattern they use.

Occasional deviations from an otherwise regular metre will cause the reader to prick up his ears. The rhythm of Kipling's poem *The White Man's Burden* is iambic throughout. But in the last stanza, where he summarizes the judgement that the Empire builders can expect from their peers at home, he introduces two spondees that fall as the strokes of a hammer: "Comes now, to search your manhood/ Through all the thankless years/ Cold, edged with dear-bought wisdom/ the Judgement of your peers." Functional rhythm occurs e.g. in Tennyson's *The Charge of the Light Brigade*: the trochees are meant to imitate the galloping of horses.

The Poetic Element

It is hardly possible to make generalizing statements about what 'the poetic element' of a poem is. That phenomenon is the result of the interaction of several factors that differ from poem to another: the structure of one poem may be due to a conflict between, rather than a cooperation of, its ingredients; another poem is remarkable for the boldness of its metaphors, a third poem makes sophisticated use of rhythm, a fourth makes the reader gasp for breath owing to the soaring flights of the poet's imagination, the profound thought of a fifth makes the reader feel dizzy, a sixth strikes the reader by the pithiness of its formulations, etc.

Drama

Title, Cast, Stage Directions

If the title page characterizes a text as tragedy or comedy, that information prompts some expectations in the reader, expectations that the teacher can draw on, and which it will be rewarding to discuss with the students. After finishing the drama, some interest will naturally be focused on the extent to which our expectations were fulfilled.

The cast, too, is likely to invite speculation, not only in regard to the individual characters, but also to the plot. An obvious assignment is to ask the students to suggest the outlines of the development of the plot and the characters on the basis of the hints given in the cast, i.e. before they read the play. Such preliminary approaches are not mere guesswork, for the stage directions may provide valuable information.

The difference between short and long stage directions is worth dwelling on. Late 19th century so-called naturalist theatre employs detailed descriptions of the characters' appearance, the arrangement of the room and, besides, gives fairly detailed information about the characters' minds, backgrounds, etc. Those facts create a detailed literary universe – Shaw' stage directions are often full-sized short stories – but at the same time as they guide the reader, they tie him hand and foot, clipping the wings of his imaginative cooperation. The speeches of especially the early parts of such dramas will often turn out to be exemplifications of the dramatist's initial comments.

Plays having short stage directions are entirely different. The dramatists who are unjustifiably called absurd often restrict themselves to giving the characters' approximate ages and the time of the day when the play is supposed to take place. The difference between the two kinds of briefing given by the playwright becomes apparent when the students are asked to perform scenes of the play, or the whole of it: if the stage directions are 'naked', a great responsibility rests on the shoulders of the actors in regard to facial expression, body language, and elocution of the speeches.

Once the reading the play has started, the reader's uncertainty is gradually reduced, and the question of the motive power of the play soon arises. Is it a conflict between two political ideologies (e.g. dictatorship vs democracy, as in Shakespeare's *Julius Caesar*)? Is it an individual's feelings (e.g. lust for power, as in *Macbeth*, or for money, as in most of the Restoration comedies)? Is it a clash of two ideologies or two generations (as in Albee's *Who Is Afraid of Virginia Woolf*)? Is it individual vs society (as in Miller's *Death of a Salesman*)? Is it social criticism or satire (as in Congreve's *The Way of the World*)? Is it dialogue drama with little action (as in T. S. Eliot's drawing-room dramas), or is it a drama with violent scenes (like Marlowe's plays)? Is it a pastiche of earlier works (like Dryden's *All for Love*)? Does the play proceed according to an inexorable inherent logic (like Sheriff's *Journey's End)*, or would it be possible for the play to go on indefinitely without seeming to get anywhere (like Beckett's *Waiting for Godot*)?

Inevitably, the situation at the end of the play will have to be compared with the opening scene: what has actually happened in the course of the play? Is the ending logical or surprising by the standards of the play's own premises? The happy ending of comedies is often less plausible than it-had-to-happen-like-that final scenes of tragedies. It is true that the villain's downfall often carries quite a number of fine, innocent people with it, but, as a genre, tragedy is realistic since far from everybody is treated after his deserts by life, and fate has a keen eye for human frailty.

Quite naturally, we gradually come to look at the technical aspect. According to Aristotle, a play should have a beginning, a middle, and an end. Does the play we are analysing live up to that standard? Is it carried forward towards its conclusion by its own momentum, or is the dénouement (i.e. the untying of the knot) brought about by extraneous forces like the *deus ex machina* who appears in many Restoration dramas: the unexpected arrival of a letter cuts many a Gordian knot in those plays.

Characters' entries and exits are never accidental, but loaded with significance, and students will find little difficulty in accounting for them once they have had their attention drawn to the function of the device. What this means is that they can acquire a fairly simple insight into an important aspect of dramatic technique.

In the early stages of their drama reading, some students may find it an obstacle that all characterization in a drama is conveyed by means of often conflicting speeches. They may need the teacher's help to get them on the track. The point is that especially young students may have some difficulty in making the mental effort that is required: the fact that a character uttering such words can be aptly characterized by means of this or that adjective, is not immediately obvious to everybody.

The drama is a suitable genre for an investigation into characters' functions in a fictional universe. It is more than just the fact that most of them develop from Act One to Act Five. Over and above that, we are given almost didactic illustrations of the difference between hero and villain, individual and type, main character and satellite, protagonist and secondary character.

Language becomes of primary importance when analysing a drama: with the kind of language they use, speakers characterize themselves. Therefore, speeches are excellent material for a study of speech acts: a sequence of words may be so formulated that, superficially, it is a question, but in actual fact it is nothing of the kind. It may be a command, a request, or an insult. This, then, is one more area where literature is a storehouse of examples of the way we use language.

It goes without saying that the problem dealt with in the play should be discussed, whether on our way through it, or at the end of our reading of it. A play practically always expresses or implies at attitude to fundamental and familiar human issues like love, hatred, honour, duty, friendship. Does the dramatist really discuss the problem, or does he just throw light on it? Does he offer some kind of solution, or is the play open-ended? Does his presentation enable us, the readers, to see his point clearly? The so-called naturalistic writers were satisfied that a problem can be discussed and solved satisfactorily in a matter of two and a half hours. In their plays, virtually every single line carries some significance for the plot or the characterization. The ending shows the untying of the knot before our eyes, and there are few, if any, loose ends. A discussion of the 'realism' of such an approach will arise almost spontaneously.

A radically different technique is seen in many modern plays. Harold Pinter, for example, keeps us (and sometimes the actors too!) in the dark as to the exact nature of the problem and the characters' backgrounds. Dialogue runs idle or is more or less incoherent, and the play does not seem to be carried forward by any inherent necessity. More often than not, the ending is puzzling; no explanation in the proper sense of the word is ever given, either to those on the stage or to the audience. Dramas tailored to that pattern are often called absurd, which seems surprising. Surely everyday dialogues and situations more often develop à la Pinter than Ibsen? Actually, many students are keenly aware of the confusing terminology, and they realize that so-called realism in the drama is a manipulation of reality.

Dramatic Irony

Dramatic irony deserves particular attention from the teacher because it is a technically interesting device. A character's speech contains some information that is fraught with consequences. The point is that the author has so arranged the development of the play that the reader or spectator will be familiar with those consequences, whereas the actor who speaks the lines is unaware of the implications. The author has established a tacit pact with his audience, a wordless dialogue that passes over the head of the speaker of the lines. The secret shared by author and audience is revealed only later in the text, but a student's task could be to ascertain when the mutual contact is brought about, to decode the message, and to isolate the means that the dramatist has made use of. Obviously, some dramatists are more elegant in their handling of the trick than others, and that, too, gives rise to discussions.

Performance

Dramas are meant to be performed, and students should be asked to try their hand on one or more of the scenes, perhaps the whole play. It is a healthy exercise, for performing will promote understanding of the way technical problems can or must be solved: attention will have to be focused on the way a phrase is to be turned, and in order for actors to speak sequences of dialogue, they must have mentally supplemented a number of 'background verbs' like shout whisper, implore, gloat, complain, and corresponding gestures and facial expressions will have to be taken into account. A director's difficulties, e.g. his need of making compromises, will become apparent.

In connection with the performance, the three unities, time, place, and action, may be discussed. In a concrete situation, it is obvious that they were more suitable for some types of play than for others. Why were the Neo-Classicists so fond of them? That will naturally lead on to a discussion of the concept of paradigms. Are they, when used in literary parlance, in actual fact 'thought prisons'?

The Novel

The novel offers unique opportunities to investigate the techniques that an author uses to create a literary universe. He has a story that he finds worth telling, and he needs a framework for it. If he wants to make his narrative plausible, he will have to somehow copy the 'real' universe; even utopias have recognizable elements. Still, in the process of transference into the world of fiction, his story will necessarily undergo some changes. The tie-up is often close, but not complete. And that is where our analysis comes in.

A novel is a self-contained system, located in terms of time and place. A fictional world respects only its own axioms; true and false acquire a meaning that may be different from what we are accustomed to; true comes to mean 'true in the context of the work'. Even though 'before/after' is valid in fiction, it often has an idiosyncratic system of logic. Breaches of our sense of logic often have functional value, and concomitant interest. The question we should ask is whether a given situation or sequence of incidents is valid, probable, or necessary in the literary universe.

If we want to benefit from, or to do justice to, the work, we must, at least initially, play the author's game. Thus his narrative will be told in the past tense, which is a conventional 'fiction indicator'. On the one hand, we can discuss or criticize the text, but if we want to be honest, the starting-point must be to take it as it is presented to us. If an author lets one of his characters die, a discussion of the work that is based on the assumption that he lived on is of course permissible, but it will 'leave' the fictional universe: fiction cannot be corrected. However, we are free to say that the author showed considerable technical clumsiness in the way he got rid of the character. And we may find it deplorable that a man or woman having such sterling qualities should suffer an untimely death. The point is that the conditions of the communication that is triggered off by the text are derived from the text itself.

The Plot

The plot is the Ariadne's thread that, after introducing us to it, guides us through the imaginary world. A plot is the result of the processing of events in an author's mind before he communicates the sequence to us, his readers.

The fact that the plot is a consciously structured series of incidents has some corollaries: first, it is possible to create several plots on the basis of the same material. That is seen, e.g. in screen versions of novels and in different ages' varying treatments of the same material. Also, an allegory can be said to have two different plots, viz. the surface account and the underlying moral. An allegory is a story which is also a story about something else. Secondly, the peculiarities of the different types of novel (e.g. the biographical, the Utopian, the picaresque, etc.) are not the effect of changes in the basic structure of the plot.

A plot is characterized by *selectivity*. Since it is neither possible nor relevant to give a complete picture of the world of the novel, the author has had to cut corners and give us a slice of life. While reading the novel, we build up a covering picture based on the author's information and suggestions, just as in our everyday life we form a total impression on the basis of fragments. Parts only acquire meanings when incorporated in larger wholes. The sentence 'The king died, and then the Queen died' does not allow us to draw any conclusions about the relationship between the two Royals. However, if the sentence runs as follows, 'The King died, and then the Queen died of sorrow!', we have an embryo of a plot because we are justified in believing that they were closely attached to each other.[6]

The problem for the author is where and how to start the novel: *ab ovo*, i.e. from the beginning, *in medias res*, i.e. in the middle of things, or at the end, as happens in detective novels? How much background information will the author find it necessary to supply in order to prompt the reader's suspension of disbelief? A novel will usually be a consecutive account, but there will invariably be some lacunae, periods of 'zero time' which are passed over lightly because the author found them of inferior significance. Can we, his readers and students, fill in those lacunae with our creative imagination? Do we understand why the author chose to cut corners?

Thus, there will be some 'stop and go' progression in the novel, but the overall rhythm is that of a drama: from exposition via complication to a climax and ensuing solution. A situation of calm at the beginning is disturbed by incipient tension, and the pattern of the novel shows how that tension is resolved. The narrative will be dominated by alterations, viz. between problem and solution, question and answer, conflict and reconciliation, expectation and satisfaction. Every incident has an opening stage and a finishing stage, which is the reason why change is a fundamental characteristic of the plot.

Pivotal Moments

Every novel contains some pivotal moments, i.e. situations that raise or answer questions. A novelist will usually take great pains to prepare the reader for the entry of the main character. Besides, pivotal moments may often depict actions or situations that are humanly or culturally significant, i.e. they point beyond the world of fiction: a woman sitting by a window is rarely in itself sufficient to trigger off action, but a woman leaving home will often be fraught with consequences. Also, when the author wants to convey his message, he arranges a pivotal moment to honour the occasion. Students might be asked to investigate how, linguistically and dramatically, the pivotal moment is structured.

Coincidences

Coincidences are the life blood of a novel, game changers that push the action forward. It may be an accidental meeting, an unexpected arrival, or a forgotten letter that suddenly and radically transform the situation in the literary universe. Sometimes coincidences are used to cut the Gordian knot when things have reached a deadlock. Coincidences are more or less plausible seen from the point of view of a person who stands outside the world of fiction. Can those we consider less successful be explained or perhaps even defended from within the universe of the book?

The Ending

As the novel approaches its final stages, we witness a reduction of the number of options open to the characters, often a speedier movement and a mounting tension; we are heading for a new kind of equilibrium, or perhaps an indissoluble dilemma. All that is reflected in the language, and here is an inviting area of study. Also the convention that a wedding between two of the parties involved ensures their happiness 'ever after' will, especially to more mature students, appear as a strange postulate, but also so much of a convention that it will be expected to happen.

Quite naturally, the situation at the ending will be compared to that which prevailed at the beginning. Has the initial scheme been implemented, or only implemented halfway – or perhaps not at all?

Rhythm

Most novels show a rhythmical progression, e.g. in the distribution of 'show' incidents and 'tell' situations. The opening pages of a novel will usually be told by the narrator because they contain some necessary background information and introduce a platform laden with possibilities. But as the book goes along, some incidents may be dramatized and 'performed' in dialogue form.

The speed of the narrative may also be influenced by successive alterations between statis and dynamism. Foremost among the static passages are *descriptions*, be it of landscapes, rooms, the weather, a character's past, or his mental operations. At first glance they may seem to be mere irritants to a reader who just wants to get on with the story. Admittedly, they slacken the speed of the narrative, and they almost invariably represent a 'tell' sequence.

On closer inspection, descriptions can nearly always be shown to have functional value. Thus, the individual description possesses an inherent interest because the placement of it is significant: it may be symbolic, a reflection of a character's mood, necessary background information, or an elaboration of items of the plot. More generally, descriptions are inserted where they are, in order to create an atmosphere – what atmosphere?

Characterization

The novel furnishes ample material for a more thoroughgoing study of the technique of fictional characterization.

In his group of characters, an author reduces a potentially infinite number of human beings to a handful of figures. By the same token, the innumerable facets of human nature are limited to a set of norms and deviations. In the individual character, the author selects some invariants from the sequence of bodily and mental changes in a human being's life. So, characterization, too, is a consequence of *selection.*

Fictional characters are provided with recognizable human features, a fact which makes them suitable material for students' discussions. Most of them are measurable by human standards, but those who are not, are not the least interesting, also to students. The condition is that they 'belong' and cohere in the book, which does not prevent them from being one-dimensional or eccentric. Also, relations between the characters are usually such as we know them from reality: they desire or reject, love or hate, betray or support, feel attracted or repelled, plus numerous other possibilities. Those factors contribute to conferring identity on the characters, and they are of decisive importance for the structure of the work.

The characters are inextricably interwoven with the plot. According to the structuralists, characters are purely functional. Brooks and Warren point out that it is often rewarding to ask, "Whose story is this?"[7] The structuralists maintain that when fictional characters have got features that are psychologically recognizable, it is due to a trick on the author's part to justify the characters' acts and make them palatable. As they see it, also acts are purely functional.

Whatever its truth value, the structuralist postulate cuts little ice with many students, because they refuse to conceive of characters in terms of pieces in a puzzle. That may be an indirect compliment to the author's success in making his characters lifelike, or, less positively, it may be taken as evidence of many students' incapacity to distinguish between fact and fiction. On the other hand, depersonalizing the fictional participants so as to make them mere puppets or agents deprives them of a good deal of their potentiality as discussion material. And the structuralists seem to have difficulty in explaining the fact that all characters in a novel are not on the same level.

In 1927, E. M. Forster established a very serviceable distinction between *flat* and *round* characters.[8] Even though the discovery of the difference may be much older than Forster, he was the man who put a name on it, the and the terminology has proved eminently useful, also pedagogically, because it helps students towards a clearer understanding of the relationship between the characters of a novel, and of the connection between plot and characters.

A flat character does not develop as the book goes along. His characteristics, which are comparatively few, are laid down once and for all. His activities are those that are expected and predictable in the book's universe. Accordingly, he is less fascinating and intriguing than e.g. the hero. A flat character is, more often than not, a secondary character, and he may come very close to the structuralist conception in so far as he is not there in his own right, but because he is needed by the plot. Oliver Twist, in Dickens' novel, is the boy to whom, or in whose presence, the string of incidents that form the plot happens.

Flat characters are sometimes mere sketches that make a momentary appearance – Dickens' gallery furnishes a host of examples. They run the risk of becoming stereotypes because only one side of their 'personality' is shown: Mrs. Bennet in Jane Austen's *Pride and Prejudice* is the proverbial nervous wreck.

Round characters are instrumental in starting the plot and, even if they may be off stage for some time, they determine the development of the narrative.

Gradually, more and more of their character is revealed; incidents of the plot may be arranged with the intention of eliciting new facets of their personality, which becomes more and more forceful. They are possessed of sterling qualities, dormant at the beginning, in full bloom at the end. And the intriguing thing is that when we close the book, we have a feeling that they may still be able to surprise us.

Another distinction that has proved theoretically as well as pedagogically fertile is that between two modes of presentation, viz. the *dramatic* (or *indirect*) one, and the *epic* (or *direct*) one. They apply in the 'show' and 'tell' episodes respectively. In the epic approach, the narrator informs us about a person's appearance or character, and about the way other people look at him. The narrator may also analyse a character's motives and establish a kind of understanding with the reader over the character's head.

In the dramatic technique, the narrator withdraws, leaving the floor for the character to convey the information required by means of direct speech, or perhaps dialogue with another fictitious character. For reasons of space not all characters can be allowed to reveal their true identity in this way.

Many of the great 19th century novelists give a number of characterizing adjectives the moment a character is sent 'on stage', and immediately afterwards the character is made to illustrate and confirm the intension of those 'anticipating' adjectives. Admittedly, the narrator manages to put his message across, but he ties the reader hand and foot, and there is little room for deviation. Therefore, many students prefer a different approach, which leaves it to the reader to establish the characterization of a participant on the basis of what he or she says or does. They find the latter approach technically superior and more challenging as a topic for debate.

Quite naturally, some characters tend to attract the reader's attention to a greater extent than others. The author has shuffled the cards so as to give prominence to one or two characters, whom he describes in greater detail than the other inhabitants of the literary universe. The hero will often be provided with, and represent, the plus values of a given age, in regard to his outward appearance as well as to his mental characteristics, a fact which will be relevant to investigate when reading texts from earlier centuries. Many heroes in 19th and 20th century novels are rewarded with money (and, consequently, a high social status) and the prettiest girl (who is a status symbol, but who can also be supposed to give our hero an enviable sex life). Heroes are usually active, they will search and they will find, but heroes can be victims, too, as is seen in the well-known European theme of the Patient Griseldis. The hero of Sassoon's poem *Represssion of War Experience* differs considerably from Thackeray's *Henry Esmond.* A study of the figure of the literary hero in different ages will be a valuable contribution to the history of culture.

The tragic hero, to whom many students feel sympathetic, is not a person of flawless virtue or provided with an incorruptible sense of justice, nor is he utterly depraved and vicious. Often, his misfortune will be brought upon him by some false step caused by human frailty.

The villain is the hero's contrast. He may show acceptable behavior at the early stages of the book, but, in retrospect, that only serves to emphasize his hypocrisy. Interest will often be centred on how he manages to cheat his surroundings, what ultimately brings about his downfall, and at what stage of the narrative he is made to reveal his true character.

In many novels, it is appropriate to talk about a

protagonist or main character rather than calling him a hero. His conduct is not automatically determined by the activities of the other characters. Whereas the hero interprets and makes syntheses (often for the benefit of the reader), the main character is often content merely to notice things and allow the reader to draw his conclusions. Hemingway's stories provide numerous examples of main characters. Bourdieu calls the type *personnages repères*[9] – second rank, but useful for specific purposes.

Other characters do not rise above the rank and file. They do not compel any great interest in their own right, and are just so many cogs in the wheel. Still, let the students try to find out what the 'wheel' would be like without one or more of them.

A very simple way to set the students thinking and to make them speak freely is to ask the following questions: (1) what does the narrator tell us, and what does he not tell us, about the character in question? (2) what does the character himself say or do or think, and what does he not say or do or think? (3) what do the other characters say and think about him, and what do they say to him? And what do the other characters not say or think about him, and what do they not do to him?

Point of View

When we talk about point of view in literature, we mean the angle from which the story is seen, or, to put it differently, we talk about the narrator's relationship to the story he is telling us. In diary novels and epistolary novels, the author pretends to be speaking in his own person, but, as a rule, the author prefers to present the material of his story via another consciousness than his own. Accordingly, the interest of point of view resides in the part played by the narrator.

The most important roles are the following: (1) the

narrator is omniscient and ubiquitous. He says more than any of the characters know, and he comments freely on what is happening in the literary universe. That is also the technique used in epic poetry. (2) The narrator limits himself to the senses and consciousness of one character. That is probably the most commonly used technique, employed from the infancy of the modern novel, in the middle of the 18th century and onwards. (3) The narrator observes and reports with complete objectivity, furnishing no insight into that which is inaccessible to the senses. The technique is found in Impressionist writers from the last quarter of the 19th century, but was given powerful impetus by behaviorism. The author hides completely behind the narrator, which means that he has no opportunity of giving private comments on the plot and the characters.

The narrator may choose to change the point of view as the narrative proceeds. Or he may experiment with the same series of incidents seen from several angles, as Laurence Durrell does in the *Alexandria Quartet*. Samuel Richardson alternated between several letter writers in *Pamela* from 1740.

For pedagogical reasons, it is practical to distinguish between two basic types of point of view, viz. the first-person and the third-person one. In stories having a first-person point of view, the narrator is actively present in the narrative; he appears as 'I' and he is either a character or an observer, and he characterizes himself by what he says or does.

The advantages of this technique, which students are generally quick to see, are that the 'I' holds the story together – the story is about what he can see, hear, feel, or think. The personal angle lends some credibility to the text. The drawbacks are the limitations it imposes; the narrator is able to give only the information he can plausibly possess, which means that his creator, the author, must take care to place him in situations that make it likely that he should know this or that.

In the third-person narrative, the narrator stands outside the literary universe. By pointing at it, he makes his reader aware of phenomena and arrangements within it. The omniscient narrator lets us into the minds of one or more characters, pretending to know what they feel or think; he remembers the past, explains the present, and anticipates the future. He is godlike in the sense that he does not explain where or how he got his information. Sometimes he may find it opportune to withhold some information, for example to achieve suspense. Since he is not in the literary universe, he will often become what might be called a 'commenting consciousness'.

Of course it is difficult for the narrator to be omniscient with many characters – in the case of long novels it is impossible. Again we see the necessity of making a selection. The character he chooses to be omniscient with will generally prove to be the main character.

The 'camera' technique is the opposite of the omniscient narrator. The 'camera' only reports words and actions, never thoughts, emotions or motives. The narrator's function becomes analogous to that of an eye-witness who happens to be present. The method lends a touch of credibility to the account.

A good approach for the teacher will be to exploit the distinction between the epic and the dramatic modes. That is significant, not only for characterization, but also for determining the narrator's role and his possibilities of informing the reader. In the dramatic mode, the narrator does not know more than the participants whose conversations he renders; successive scenes are 'performed' before the reader's eyes; in the epic mode, the narrator knows more than the reader: he records *and* informs.

Motif and Theme

A motif is an item *in* the text, the theme is an abstract idea *deduced from* the text. A motif is a verbalized feature that recurs frequently in the work or in parts of the work, often as an accompaniment to decisive passages in the narrative, or to one of the characters' moods. The weather is a motif frequently used to symbolize a character's state of mind (e.g. in *Wuthering Heights*). That use of the weather is an instance of what T. S. Eliot called 'the objective correlative'.[10] The repetitions are rarely verbatim ones, but still the slightly varied formulations become one of the constants of the text, one of its supporting pillars.

Since motifs are empirically verifiable, students will generally not find it difficult to trace them. They are also 'pedagogic' in the sense that they point beyond the mere words, conferring 'depth' on the narrative. Thus they may contribute to clarifying the reader's grasp of the text in that they are landmarks in his progressive reading. They tend to strengthen the reader's understanding of the structure of the work and also give increased insight into the message of the text.

The theme is not an incident or a cluster of words that appear in the text, and the reader cannot identify the theme by adding up some of the elements of the text; for example, the theme is not equivalent to the sum of motifs. The theme is not concrete information about the characters' lives and activities. Rather, it is the name given to the general idea that can be derived from the work as a whole, the view of life and the world that unifies and permeates the narrative. It is an abstraction above word level, words raised to the second power, so to speak.

When we attempt to isolate the theme (or themes: a work may have more than theme), we engage in an undertaking that is reminiscent of what happens in interpretation. In both cases, we must rise above the components of the text and make a pattern of them, thus getting at the ultimate idea and unity of the text. Though not essentially moralistic, themes come very close to being illustrations of some of life's 'general laws'.

The theme is connected with the macrostructure of the work. One definition of the quality of a literary work might be to say that a valuable text is one whose themes are weighty, fascinating, disgusting, or in other respects worthy of attention and interest. A substantial text is one that, in the opinions of mature and sensible human beings, says something significant. Unfortunately, not every valuable text is appropriate teaching material, and teaching cannot limit itself to dealing with texts of sterling merit.

The remarkable fact is that we may all come to find a text valuable without approving of its theme. It seems to be a common human experience that we can feel attracted by stories that we find abhorrent – in the same way as we can be strangely fascinated by people we dislike intensely. Even if the theme is objectionable – or perhaps for the very reason that *is* objectionable – the text may be worth discussing The theme of Doris Lessing's *The Good Terrorist* is the obvious danger of laid-back, blind naiveté. When a text seems insipid or worthless, it is often because its theme is trivial or unconvincing. The important thing is the way the story "puts the idea and, in the process of living, modifies the idea".[11] Students may sometimes need some help, but once they get the hang of it, they enjoy it – often so much so that the teacher must interfere to stop the work deteriorating onto mere treasure hunting.

Themes will often epitomize basic human situations and conditions, and they tend to cluster in pairs or contrasts: town vs country, youth vs. old age (frequently in the form of innocence vs. experience), an individual's ideals vs. the conventions (or demands) of society, illusion vs. reality, the conflict between social classes, etc. The contrasts may – especially in the early stages of the text – appear incompatible, and the book will describe if and how the opposites are reconciled.

A consequence of this universality is that themes are not reserved to works written in one language. Actually, most themes are the common property of several European literatures. Thus, the theme of the 'personal initiation', about the youth who sets off from home to be tested by the world, is perhaps the most frequently recurring theme in 19th and 20th century European literatures.

Other shared themes are *carpe diem* (gather ye rose-buds while ye may, or strike while the iron is hot), *ubi sunt* (Oh, what a falling off was there), the *Prometheus* theme (about the presumptuous human being who was foolhardy enough to try to wring the fire from the gods). Some are named after the fictional characters that have come to stand as their most evident and prominent exponents (further evidence of the intimate relationship between fact and fiction): *Faustus* (the man who sells his soul to the devil in return for worldly wisdom and power); *Don Juan* (the heartless seducer who is in the end caught up by his destiny); *Don Quixote* (the well-intentioned but naïve idealist, whose fighting spirit is wasted on trifles and misun-derstandings); *Robinson Crusoe* (Defoe's version, not Campe's) (the man who is marooned on a desert island, but who remains undaunted and is ultimately victorious thanks to his skill and stamina); *Romeo and Juliet* (two passionate young lovers, whose love ends in a catastrophe).

It is not a straightforward job to 'teach themes' because a theme envelops a text in its entirety, and because it is an abstraction that cannot be reached by a simple process of addition. Many students are a bit reluctant to 'let go their hold of the text', as they put it, and start floating in midair. So, the inductive teaching method, which aims at eliciting something that is latent in the students, will have to be replaced by a teacher-directed guidance. Most students cannot be expected to be familiar with all the great European masterpieces. So, this is one of the areas where teaching of literature means communication of knowledge, which is, of course, one of its functions.

A word of warning is appropriate. the teaching of literature should not lapse into an empty pursuit of motifs and themes. It is with the latter two as with stylistic features: the decisive thing is not the fact that a modern writer makes use of the Don Juan theme, but how he exploits it.

CHAPTER NINE

Sticking Points: Value, Evaluation, the Literary Experience

Value, experience and evaluation are delicate subjects to handle. In order to be able to express, and be justified in expressing, opinions with any degree of authority in those fields, a person must have a considerable amount of life experience and literary training. Matters are further complicated by the fact that the three concepts seem to be completely arbitrary and idiosyncratic. However, on this point it is important not to allow oneself to be blindfolded by the pretended objectivity of science.

There is little doubt that the humanities suffer from a massive inferiority complex vis-à-vis science as far as validity and reliability are concerned. The laws of science are seen as the ultimate illustrations of objectivity. When a math problem 'works out', there is often an end of it, and there are no loose ends. But no matter how you tackle a literary text, it can hardly ever achieve the same remainder-less solution. The more deeply you delve into a valuable literary text, the more reservations and additions you will be forced to make. And in spite of all your efforts to hedge your bets ('However' . . . , 'But then again' . . . , or 'On the other hand' . . .), there will always, apart from strictly biographical information, be something left hanging in the air. It would be absurd to use math-like objectivity as the benchmark, because the air of finality surrounding much of science is not the *ambiance* of literature. Besides, the more complicated problems within math sometimes admit of different solutions, exemplifying varying degrees of elegance and sophistication on top of their truth value. So, subjectivity comes in by the back door. It is characteristic that the plays of Ibsen and his school, which seemingly cut the Gordian knot and dispose of the initial problem, are contemporaneous with the halcyon days of Positivism.

A pretty commonplace conclusion would be that statements concerning value, experience, and evaluation are in actual fact nothing but so many value judgements. But subjectivity does not have to be synonymous with utter arbitrariness. It is of decisive significance who gives the verdict. It is a legitimate assumption that a reader who is familiar with the outlines of aesthetic history from the Renaissance and onwards, and whose reading has made him sensitive to the factors that make a literary work an artifact (let's call him the teacher!), will always be worth listening to. He may not always be right, but any mistakes he may commit are likely to be genuinely interesting.

The varying conceptions of taste that have dominated different ages have, to a considerable extent, been products of subjectivism. What happened was that the majority of competent and intelligent critics of a given age largely agreed on what was good and what was bad. In questions of value and evaluation, we witness a considerable amount of consensus among the influential literati of a period. The 'intersubjectivity', as it might be called, interpreted, or was based on, some criteria that were commonly agreed to be fundamental, but those criteria, the 'rules' for good and correct writing, changed from one period to another. The Neo-Classicists thought that, to be accepted, literature should imitate classical precedents like Homer and Vergil. The Romanticists, discarding imitation as a criterion, held that literature should be sincere, i.e. make the poet's feelings manifest. It is important to inform the students that such criteria are man-made, hence temporary, not instituted by God.

If the students are to be enabled to carry on a reasonably sensible conversation about value and evaluation, they must be taught the definitions and implications of a series of technical terms. To mention a few examples: overriding concepts like composition, symbol, and metaphor; genre-dependent terms like stanza, metre and rhythm within poetry; monologue, dialogue, stage direction, and dénouement within drama; coincidence, *ab ovo, in medias res* within the novel. The aim is not to enable the students to play ping-pong with the terms of a technical jargon, and it is obviously unfortunate if technical terminology replaces insight, or perhaps even blocks understanding. Technical terms should be looked upon exclusively in terms of a short-cut to unambiguous communication.

Value

For several reasons, value is not an easy thing to handle – inside as well as outside the classroom. Value judgements are subjective, but some are better argued than others. When a person says "This text is valuable," he may mean valuable to himself or valuable by general consensus. Those two need not be identical. If I may make a personal confession, Spenser's *Fairie Queene* has never set my enthusiasm aflame. But the poem is, by general consensus, agreed to be of high quality. Not all verdicts on Homer coincide, but the majority of influential critics have found his works a worth-while object of study.

Furthermore, long texts are not valuable from cover to cover. James Thomson's *The Seasons* contains a lot of splendid passages, but also a good deal of claptrap. Still, considered in its entirety, it remains a valuable work. It would be impossible to make a list of indispensable features that invariably confer value a text. Yet European literatures show that 'great themes' have a greater chance to produce texts of high quality than more ephemeral subjects. Texts describing man's relationship to his neighbour, to his God, and to himself, nature in its charming or frightening aspects, religion as an awe-inspiring force, have sparked off a good many literary masterpieces.

The outcome of 'teaching values' is – hopefully – that, by slow degrees, students will begin to know what to look for in a text, and to make more sophisticated demands on a text if they are to recognize it as valuable. They will become aware that some texts trigger many ideas and seem almost inexhaustible whereas others can be finished off in the twinkling of an eye. Some texts provide them with staggering or disturbing insight (literature is news that remains news), whereas others tell them little more than they knew beforehand; some texts are formally successful (which is not synonymous with smooth and regular), whereas others are mere torsos (which is not automatically synonymous with failures). A poet's elegant handling of a metre, a story writer's pithy use of metaphors, a novelist's command of huge panoramas will captivate students more and more. Slowly, the students' scale of values undergoes a change, and as they become more and more experienced readers, they will become increasingly aware of the inherent interest of the combination of content and form. They will have been given tools to fit the work that is being discussed into a larger context. Actually, many students are astonished to see that contemporary literature has strong technical and aesthetic bonds with much that precedes it.

Two interesting criteria of aesthetic value that are comprehensive also in the sense that they reach beyond our own age have been formulated by the prominent Danish literary critic, Professor Bent Sunesen, in his seminal book *Towards a Theory of Foreign-Language Literature Teaching*.[1]

Expandability is the fact that the work is capable of bursting the fetters of a one-track and doctrinaire interpretation. The implications are that a work may contain more than meets the eye, and that different ages can read different things into a work. For instance, it is a well-known fact that successive generations have had divergent attitudes to Milton. Sunesen's theory also accounts for the fact that an author who is a visionary genius may be ahead of his age by intuitively grasping problems that were not made explicit until much later. Huxley's *Brave New World* could be cited as an example. Finally, the criterion is satisfactory because it allows one work to be susceptible of several interpretations that are equally acceptable.

The second criterion, viz. *empatheticity*, indicates that a work has aesthetic value if it invites the reader to be absorbed in it and be empathetic towards it. It implies that different readers can benefit in different, legitimate ways from the reading of the same work.

The two criteria exclude literary snobbism, while at the same time recognizing that some works are better than others. They acknowledge the fact that the connoisseur has the possibility of penetrating more deeply into a text than the neophyte. Besides, the criteria do not establish extraneous rules which a work has to observe. Within the framework of the theory, value becomes an issue to be settled between work and reader, which means that the theory has some affinity with the assumptions of the Reader Response Criticism.

Evaluation

Reflections on the aesthetic value of a work and formulations of aesthetic experiences will almost invariably lead to evaluations of the work. 'Value' and 'evaluation' are closely related in more than their verbal representation. The utility of evaluations is a function of the possibility of substantiating them. There is not, and probably will never be, a universal and unequivocal theory that is capable of explaining why one work is outstanding, and another one mediocre.

Why is *King Lear* a better play than George Lillo's *The London Merchant* from 1731? With its wide scope, *Lear* strikes deep chords in any reader or spectator, and its theme sparks off much thinking activity. Add to this, its form is intriguing. Those points make the drama 'good' – and appropriate teaching material. Lillo's drama is far more limited and less provocative. Its form is nothing out of the ordinary. That does not in itself make it a bad play, but the 18th century bourgeois ideal that it propounds does not engage and fascinate today's students to the same extent as does Shakespeare's drama.

With the individual reader, evaluation appears as value judgements. Northrop Frye goes so far as to say that the qualities we think we are able to find in a literary work, are often just qualities that we appreciate.[2] The significance of talented instinctive verdicts should certainly not be underrated, and in the hands of shallow-brained philistines any evaluation, no matter how solid its criteria may seem to be, will often degenerate into dull pedantry. However, as everybody knows, intuitively graspable messages from the Land of Genius arrive very sporadically, and are only bestowed on a small minority of human beings. Accordingly, a sensible teacher will be well advised not to expect to find them in his students with great frequency.

The teacher's task, then, will be to provide his students with some tools and some knowledge so as to enable them to build their verdicts on a fairly solid basis. Having opinions, and expressing them, is of course unobjectionable, but they are not necessarily made less valuable by deriving from a solid fund of knowledge. The quality of a person's evaluations is directly proportional to his insight. As far as literature is concerned, insight may, for example, mean familiarity with some important literary conventions and techniques.

The aim must be for the students to get further than 'I like this' or 'That is rubbish', and to analyse to what extent the author has delivered. In our textual work, we use a series of value-laden terms, e.g. good, bad, successful, sentimental, banal, thought-provoking, pathetic, disgusting, etc. They all refer to our reaction to the totality of the work, but in order to get below the surface we can try to give synonyms for them in the context where they appear. The word 'good' in the syntagm 'a good man' may mean helpful, generous, Christian, faithful, moral, loving, careful, nice, plus probably something more. All experience goes to show that the man who knows 300 words fares better in the world than the man who knows only 100.

For practical reasons, evaluative criteria can be subdivided into three categories depending on their object, viz. content, form, and time. As far as content is concerned, we can talk about 'a sentimental story', 'an unsuccessful Utopia', 'a fresh version of the theme town vs. country'. Under the heading of form, we can talk about 'a banal plot', 'a well-made play', 'a sophisticated variation of the sonnet form'. Within the category of time, we can assess whether content and/or form were a novel departure, still in current use, or old wine on old bottles. Relevant terms will here be 'original', 'hackneyed', 'obsolete'. But also statements like 'a typically Romantic expression' imply a temporal aspect. Such statements may be either positive or negative. For example, 18th century writers had a different view of 'nature' than many later writers. And much to the students' surprise, a text may pass muster even if it puts forward an objectionable message: that often happens in the case of Ezra Pound's verse.

What we do, then, is to ascertain a fact, e.g. the form of the sonnet we have before our eyes, and supplement it with an evaluating epithet that places it on a relative scale. If we are to be able to call an author's use of the sonnet form 'sophisticated', we must have a standard of reference that is founded on some amount of familiarity with other poets' use of that form: that will show us where the sophistication is. Knowing the Robinson Crusoe theme is a necessary prerequisite for being able to characterize a work treating the theme as a bold venture. The variation might e.g. make Friday the main character, placing Robinson's ethical standards in a light that differs from what we are accustomed to see: Adrian Mitchell's *Man Friday* shows that inversion of the familiar theme. These are the premises of a discussion, and it will be up to the individual reader to characterize the variation as elegant or unsuccessful. The knowledge that is indispensable for a person if he is going to give a verdict cannot be acquired in a few hours on a summer afternoon in a hammock on the terrace. Elbow grease and a good deal of time are needed.

The aim should be to enable the students to verbalize their own response to a text. However, as every reader will know from his own experience, now and then we come across texts that mean something to us which it is almost impossible to put into words. For instance the text may throw us into bewilderment, or it may evoke a particular, clearly felt, but indefinable, mood. The essential thing, however, is to teach the students to stuff vague and all-inclusive verdicts like 'good' and 'bad'. Is the work 'bad' because the ending is inconclusive, because the rhythm is monotonous, because the thought is disgusting, because the main character remains a postulate, etc.? Is the work 'good' because the plot is exciting, because the characters are true to life, because the theme is of more than ephemeral interest, because the verses sound melodious when read aloud, etc.?

It is not a bad idea to finish the treatment of a work with a few words about the factors on which professional critics have based their verdict. Do we disagree entirely, or do we think they have a point? If we are lucky, the students will see the point of going deeply into a text, probably more deeply than our shared efforts took us. Nobody is going to challenge anybody's right to give an evaluation even if it seems insufficient when measured by the standards of the experts. But then again, nobody will maintain that a rather meagre assessment of a great work is necessarily the final word in the treatment of the text.

The Literary Experience

Ideally speaking, in literature facts are only the means. The end is for the acquired factual knowledge provided by literary works to inspire factors latent in the reader's mind and imagination so as to produce what is called a literary experience.

According to Northrop Frye, "works of literature are not things to be contemplated but powers to be absorbed."[3] That may be true, but in pedagogy it is not sufficient to know the goal; we must also try to become familiar with the route to follow in order to get to the goal. In other words, once more we must divide in the hope of being ultimately able to conquer. But the tricky thing is that 'experience' is something unique, and it is far from easy to isolate its constituent parts. It is a synthesis rather than a sum of clear-cut, discrete elements.

The meaning of a text can be extracted from the text. Thus, it is possible to make a prose paraphrase of a poem. That meaning is verifiable, for in cases of doubt we can compare with the text, which means that, with slight deviations, different readers will usually get approximately the same understanding of it. The intellectual element of understanding is intimately connected with something else: the reader may, for example, feel satisfaction at having put things in their proper places, memories may be evoked, a chain of associations started; he may get a spontaneous and not easily decomposable sense of the richness of the poem as compared with the meagre paraphrase. After finishing the text, the reader may come to feel that he has passed beyond the stage of 'mere understanding', which is tantamount to saying that literary works are capable of giving their reader 'something more', some kind of experience. It is the kind of impression that may leave an indelible and perhaps permanent stamp on his mind.

The experience, which is usually more intense when we read fiction than when we read non-fiction, is inseparable from the reading of the text. It 'occurs' continuously during the perusal, and it is the crowning glory when the reader closes the book after the last page. It is based on, and dependent on, an analysis of the meaning. But it says something, and provides something, that an investigation of the meaning is unable to offer. The literary experience is empirically verifiable, witness children's reaction when they are listening to a good story. The experience is the private property of the individual reader, who, of course, is free to share and discuss it with other readers – one more reason why literature is a worth-while teaching object. But the great leap into the bliss of a literary experience is the recipient's (in our situation, the student's) own responsibility: the teacher may prepare the material and open the students' eyes to some profound and relevant aspects of the text, but he cannot take his students the whole way.

The kind and degree of the student's experience are determined by permanent as well as transitory factors. His open-mindedness during the process of reading, .i.e. a temporary factor, certainly plays a part. A person may be looking forward to a concert for weeks, and when the day comes, his mind will be very impressionable. A book is capable of so engrossing a reader's attention that he forgets everything around him.

Among the permanent factors, which of course change from one individual to another, are the recipient's temperament and his biography in the widest sense of the word, i.e. his background, his memories, his intellectual make-up, and, more generally, the way things have panned out for him. A good love poem is likely to start more vibrations in an amorous teenager than in a sedate old-age pensioner. However, it is unlikely to leave the elderly person entirely cold, for, as Proust and others have shown, literary experiences have a peculiar power of making the past come alive.

The literary experience has a strong emotional ingredient: we enjoy the suspense of an exciting story, and we are captivated by an obsessive rhythm. The emotion may have an intellectual basis, as when we come to respect the artist's struggle with the medium and the mark he has left on the form. But over and above everything, there is a stronger determinant that might be called transcendent, because it widens our intellectual horizon and deepens our emotional fullness. By the way he treats universal situations and conditions as reflected in the individual manifestation, the artist gives us glimpses of the multiplicity of life and the essential community of mankind.

A teacher cannot 'teach' experience in the same way as he can teach the correct use of the relative pronouns. He is naturally powerless where the 'permanent factors' in the students' personality referred to above are concerned. What he can do, however, is to make an effort to arrange the material in such a way that his students' chances of getting beyond mere reading are increased. He can try to open his students' minds to an awareness of what words can do to people. He may point to some of the facts in the work that break the bounds of his own horizon, and in many cases he will be able to help his students put their own experience into words.

That should not lead the students to feel that the teaching is a matter of mass suggestions or a religious conversion, the point of which is to make the entire group see the light at all costs. The teacher is not necessarily a bad teacher even if all his students are not in a more or less permanent state of exultation whenever he takes them through a literary work. The point is rather that the teacher should do his best not to stand in his students' way. It is a fact that every reader has a possibility of getting some kind of thrill, be it ever so modest, during his meeting with literature. The teacher's job is to help every student part of the way.

Since meaning analysis is a prerequisite of the literary experience, it is a good idea to tackle the meaning of the text as the first step. When we are to characterize the experience, we must often have recourse to metaphoric expressions like richness, depth, scope. One of the teacher's greatest challenges is to see how far he can get without spoon-feeding the students, or without pontificating. Experience shows that it is a rewarding method to allow the students to express their reactions and give their verdicts independently and spontaneously, and to assist them with clarifying questions. Needless to say, that approach requires a sophisticated question technique because in such situations the intuitive proceeding may lead to a goal the teacher cannot have prepared.

Conclusion

Seeing how difficult it is for the practitioners and critics of music and *les beaux arts* to rise above some very down-to-earth reflections, or how easily they get lost in airy gobbledygook when they are asked to outline their goals and their working procedures to the uninitiated, one may have some misgivings with regard to the possibility of *teaching* an artistic subject. As everybody knows, it is easier to understand an explanation than to explain an understanding. Bourdieu's pronouncement that "the object of any work of art is nothing but the properly artistic way of perceiving the world"[1] is obscurity at a remove hidden behind a value judgement: a special kind of vision is claimed to be indispensable for anyone who wants to join the game.

At first sight, things seem even more complicated as far as literature is concerned. It uses language as a medium, and in literary pedagogy language comes to serve three functions: first, it is the dress of the author's thoughts, secondly, it is the tool we make use of when we are to express the meaning of a work; and, thirdly, it is the medium we use when, on a higher level, we are to verbalize our opinion and experience of the literary work.

Would it not be preferable to stop when the book has exerted its spontaneous influence on the reader? That is arguable, for such spontaneity rarely does full justice either to the work or to the author's efforts. If a teacher makes it a habit to leave books in a state of unspoiled virginity, he is a disgrace to his profession, but, more than that, he misses an excellent opportunity of talking with other people about a worth-while subject. A text is eminently a meeting-place for human minds. What is more, that teacher will demonstrate a certain amount of arrogance, implying that literature is not the province of ordinary people – it is a cult, a temple service which is the prerogative of ministrants who are familiar with the details of the ritual.

However, literature should not be put away in a curiosity shop to be duly admired, but certainly not touched. Literature is something that can and should be talked about, criticized and evaluated, and the debates can, to a considerable extent, start on a basis of common sense, a faculty which, as everyone knows, it is always most unwise to suspend.

Undergoing education means learning something about the process of learning things. The learner acquires professional knowledge, but, over and above that, he is also going through a process of socialization. The learner finds himself, understands himself better, and comes to see himself as a beginner and later as more of a student. In its origin, liberal education was understood as the opposite of scientific education. Liberal education will prevent the learner from becoming a nerd, and it also contributes to the shaping of his personality. To be operative, liberal education requires an aesthetic space, and if you strip the student's progress in the humanities of the aesthetic/ philosophic aspect, you will risk ending up in cultural barbarism.

The teacher's task is to convert his own sense of texts into serviceable pedagogy, which often means to turn the statements of a text into questions to his students. Any teacher is privileged in that he is given immediate and often unambiguous response from his students, which means that he will very quickly realize whether his level of teaching is behind, abreast of, or ahead of his students, and he can calibrate his procedures accordingly. Ideally speaking, the teacher should be able to communicate his own fascination without losing sight of the complexity of his material.

Literary pedagogy is subjective, it will be argued. Yes, of course, but so is all pedagogy – and is there any alternative? The great majority of students need help, for all experience goes to show that the alternative to a teacher-inspired interpretation is – no interpretation. That is not the end of the world, but if some people want to penetrate more deeply into the mysteries of a text, it would seem to be obvious that a person who knows something about how to use the tools of the trade, is enabled to share his knowledge and experience with those who are hungry for more. The essential thing is that the teacher does not floor his students with his own expertise, or cow them into submission with his authority. Pedagogy is neither brain-washing nor regimentation. The ideal is for things to grow organically from scratch, or from a level where everybody has the possibility of putting his oar in. As I.A. Richards pointed out, knowledge is growledge.

There is no denying that the waters of a teacher of literature are murky. One danger is that teaching is reduced to a formula, following the same procedure with all texts, and requiring all texts to meet the same demands. If the interpretative grid remains unchanged, the students' active participation is hampered, discussion is blanketed, and too many nuances are likely to be overlooked. Professionally weak teachers are likely to fall into that trap.

Another aberration is to reduce literature to a parlour game with rules so slack that almost any contribution from the students will be accepted. The winner of the game will be the person who can think of a slick and startling answer which may have a platonic relationship to the day's text. Within the framework of such a pastime, textual criticism will become a non-committal hodge-podge of a chatty summary, with a few spots of close reading added, and spiced with biographical information of a predominantly anecdotal or sensational character. Genuine penetration of the text is unobtainable.

No doubt some readers of this book will feel that it makes great demands on a teacher. Perhaps it will be more correct to say that the learning and teaching of literature are exacting disciplines to their practitioners, irrespective of whether they find themselves behind or before the teacher's desk. As I said in the Preface, the procedures suggested in the book should not be gone through relentlessly to the bitter end, and in the case of every single text. That is made impossible by the time available and the students' level – not to speak of the threshold of their patience. Nor is the teacher supposed to be a sort of jack-of-all trades who has a thousand tricks up his sleeve. I have been at great pains not to establish ultimate demands or to build an unduly simple or schematic framework for the way a teacher could tackle this or that text or this or that subject, the more so as every experienced teacher will know that the subtlest touches on the instrument are intuitive. And when all is said and done, pedagogic intuition is something that you have or do not have. Every teacher can strive to get closer to the ideal, but in the hands of the brilliant teacher teaching becomes an art.

My purpose of writing this book was twofold: first, to show that literature repays the efforts that are needed for a more than superficial preoccupation with it. Secondly, and no less importantly, I want to say this: if the teachers within the humanities are to be taken seriously, they have to show that they are specialists within their own branch, and that life would be poorer, and humanity's prospects bleaker, without their effort. They can do something valuable just as specialists within other branches can do within theirs. Thanks to his professional background and his pedagogic expertise, the teacher of literature is able to work rationally as well as intuitively with a text, and he can widen his fellow citizens' horizons by affording them some insight into the thing called art. It is a profoundly satisfactory pursuit, and one that may perhaps even win favour with The Powers That Be so that they do not identify man and his potentialities with the computer and its potentialities.

It has not been my intention to stack one utopian claim on top of another, or to oblige with shallow fireside chat. I have of course consulted relevant Church Fathers, but mostly I have drawn on my own experience. I have tried all the things that are mentioned in this book – at different times, with different categories of students, and with varying degrees of success.

I have tried to point to the stars, and I hope that, at least sometimes, my students have seen more than my finger.

Notes

CHAPTER ONE

1 *Poetics*, ed. Moxon, p. 20.
2 Bourdieu, *Les règles de l'art . . .* , p. 27.
3 *What Fiction Means*, p. 27.
4 *Biographia Literaria*, ch. xiv.

CHAPTER TWO

1 *Bacon's Essays*, ed. with Introduction and Notes by F.G. Selby, pp. 128–9.
2 *Time in Literature*, pp. 132–42.
3 *Ecclesiastes*, 1,8.
4 Walsh, *A Human Idiom*, p. 17.

CHAPTER THREE

1 George Steiner, 'Whorf, Chomsky, and the Student of Literature' in Steiner, *On Difficulty*, p. 143.
2 For an exhaustive treatment of Imagism, see Flemming Olsen, *Between Positivism and T.S. Eliot: Imagism and T.E. Hulme*, University Press of Southern Denmark 2008.
3 *The Educated Imagination*, p. 24.

CHAPTER FOUR

1 *Institutio oratoria*.
2 *Bacon's Essays*, ed. Selby, pp. 86–87.
3 Michel Riffaterre, *Essais de stylistique structurale*, p. 264.
4 *How to Read a Page*, p. 207.
5 Jonathan Culler, *Structuralist Poetics*.
6 Stanley Fish, *Is There a Text in This Class?*, p. 272.
7 Stanley Fish, *Is There a Text in This Class?*, pp. 227–35.

8 Reader, how do I please thee? Reader, how dost thou please me?
9 Charles Sanders Peirce, *Chance, Love, and Logic. Philosophical Essays*, New York 1968.
10 John R. Searle, *Speech Acts: An Essay in the Philosophy of Language*, Cambridge 1969.
11 *Conflict, Arousal, and Curiosity*, New York and London 1960.
12 *Conflict, Arousal, and Curiosity*, p. 233.

CHAPTER FIVE

1 See e.g. Jonathan Culler, 'Prolegomena to a Theory of Reading' in Suleiman & Crosman (eds.), *The Reader in the Text*, pp. 58 et seq.
2 Paul Ricoeur, *Le conflit des interprétations*, p. 16.

CHAPTER SIX

1 Bent Nordhjem, *What Fiction Means*, p. 30.
2 Wolfgang Iser, 'Interaction between Text and Reader' in Suleiman & Crosman (eds.), *The Reader in the Text*, pp. 111–112.
3 T.A.Moxon (ed.), *Aristotle's Poetics*, p. 14.
4 See e.g. Gerald Prince, 'Notes on the Text as Reader' in Suleiman & Crosman (eds.), *The Reader in the Text*, pp. 227–228.

CHAPTER SEVEN

1 *Les règles de l'art . . .* , p. 427.
2 *The Living Principle*, p. 36.
3 Penguin ed., p. 36.
4 *Language and Mind*, p. 74.
5 *Le conflit des interprétations*, p. 16.
6 David Bleich, *Subjective Criticism*, pp. 151 et seq.
7 *Les mots et les choses*, p. 171.
8 For Husserl's thought, see *Ideen zu einer Phänomenologie und phänomenologischen Philosophie*, 1993.
9 *The Structure of Scientific Revolutions*, Chicago 1962.
10 *Validity in Interpretation*, Yale 1967.

11 *Is There a Text in This Class?*, pp. 260 et seq.
12 Farrar, Strauss & Giroux 1966.
13 *The ut pictura poesis Tradition and English Neo-Classical Landscape Poetry*, University Press of Southern Denmark 2013.
14 *Art and Illusion*, Princeton 1960.

CHAPTER EIGHT

1 *Is There A Text in This Class?*, pp. 108–109.
2 *The Philosophy of Literary Form*, p. 140 et seq.
3 *The Philosophy of Literary Form*, p. 142.
4 *Essais de stylistique structurale*, p. 145.
5 *Poetics*, ed. Moxon, p. 45.
6 The Example is given in Forster, *Aspects of the Novel.*
7 *Understanding Fiction*, p. 171.
8 *Aspects of the Novel.*
9 *Les règles de l'art . . .*, p. 21.
10 See Flemming Olsen, *Eliot's Objective Correlative. Tradition or Individual Talent*, Sussex Academic Press 2012.
11 Brooks & Warren, *Understanding Fiction*, pp. xvii–xviii.

CHAPTER NINE

1 Copenhagen, Danmarks Lærerhøjskole 1975.
2 *The Stubborn Structure*, p. 71.
3 *The Stubborn Structure*, p. 82.

CONCLUSION

1 *Les règles de l'art . . .*, p. 412.

Bibliography

Abercrombie, D., *Problems and Principles*. Longman 1957.

Aristotle, *Poetics,* ed. T.A. Moxon. Everyman's Library, Dent 1943.

Atwell, Nancie, *In the Middle: Writing, Reading, and Learning with Adolescents*. Portsmouth, NH: Boynton 1987.

Austin, J.L., *How to Do Things with Words*. Oxford 1962.

Bacon, *Essays*, ed. F.G. Selby. Macmillan, London 1948.

Baker, Sheridan, *The Compleat Stylist*. New York: Crowell 1966.

Barnett, R.A., *Improving Higher Education*. Buckingham. SRHE and Open University Press 1992.

Barthes, Roland, *Le Plaisir du texte*. Paris 1973.

Bergonzi, Bernard, *The Situation of the Novel*. London 1970.

Berlyne, D.E., *Conflict, Arousal, and Curiosity*. New York & London 1960.

Bjørk, L., Knight, M., Wikborg, E., *The Writing Process. Composition Writing for University Students*. Studentlitteratur, Lund, Sweden 1992.

Bleich, David, *Subjective Criticism*. Johns Hopkins University Press 1978.

Bourdieu, Pierre, *Les règles de l'art. Génèse et structure du champs littéraire*. Editions du Seuil, Paris 1992.

Booth, Wayne C., *The Rhetoric of Fiction*. Chicago University Press 1961.

Brémond, Claude, *Logique du récit*. Paris 1973.

Brooks, Cleanth, *The Well-Wrought Urn*. London 1949.

Brooks, Cleanth & Penn Warren, Robert, *Understanding Poetry*. New York 1955.

Brooks, Cleanth & Penn Warren, Robert, *Understanding Fiction*. New York 1959.

Brown, Roger, *Words and Things: An Introduction to Language*. Glencoe Free Press 1958.

Burke, Kenneth, *The Philosophy of Literary Form*. University of California Press, 3rd ed. 1973.

Chabrol, Claude et al., *Sémiotique narrative et textuelle*. Paris 1973.

Chatman Seymour (ed.), *Literary Style: A Symposium*. Oxford University Press 1971.

Chatman, Seymour, *Story and Discourse: Narrative Structures in Fiction and Film*. Cornell University Press 1978.

Chomsky, Noam, *Language and Mind*. New York 1968.

Cohen, Jean, *Structure du langage poétique*. Paris 1966.

Cooles, William and Vopat, James, *What Makes Writing Good*. Lexington, Mass.: Heath 1985.

Crowley, Sharon, *A Teacher's Introduction to Deconstruction*. Urbana: NCTE 1989.

Crystal, David & Davy, Derek, *Investigating English Style*. Longman 1969.

Culler, Jonathan, *Structuralist Poetics: Structuralism, Linguistics, and the Study of Literature*. Cornell University Press 1975.

Dalton, Stephanie Stoll & Sharp, Roland G., '*Standards for Pedagogy: Research, Theory, and Practice*' in Wells, G. & Claxton, G., *Learning for Life in the 21st Century. Sociocultural Perspectives on the Future of Education*. Oxford: Blackwell 2002, pp. 181–194.

Duncan-Audrade, M.R. & Morell, Ernest, *The Art of Critical Pedagogy: Possibilities for Moving from Theory to Practice in Urban High-School Classroom*. Peter Lang. Series Counterpoints 2008.

Dillon, George, *Language Processing and the Reading of Literature: Towards a Model of Comprehension*. Bloomington: Indiana University Press 1978.

Dubois, J., Edeline F., Klinkenberg, J.M. & Minguet, Ph., 'Lecture du poème et isotopies multiples'. *Le francais moderne*, juillet 1974.

Eagleton, Terry, *Marxism and Literary Criticism*. London 1976.

Ehrmann, Jacques (ed.), *Structuralism*. New York 1966.

Empson, William, *Seven Types of Ambiguity*. London 1930.

Empson, William, *The Structure of Complex Words*. London 1951.

English Language, Literature, and Composition: Essays and Pedagogy Study Guide. Praxis Study Guides. Educational Testing Service 2003.

Escarpit Roger, *Sociologie de la littérature*. Paris 1960.

Fish, Stanley, *Is There a Text in This Class? The Authority of Interpretative Communities*. Harvard University Press 1980.

Fokhema, Donne Wessel & Elrud, Kunne Ibsch, *Theories of Literature in the Twentieth Century: Structuralism, Marxism, Aesthetics of Reception*. New York 1978.

Forster, E.M., *Aspects of the Novel*. London 1927.

Foucault, Michel, *Les mots et les choses. Une archéologie des sciences humaines*. Paris 1966.

Fowler, Roger, *Style and Structure in Literature*. Cornell University Press 1973.

Frye, Northrop, *The Educated Imagination*. Bloomington 1964.

Frye, Northrop, *The Anatomy of Criticism*. New York 1965.

Frye, Northrop, *The Stubborn Structure*. New York 1974.

Fuller, T., *The Voice of Liberal Learning*. London & New Haven, Yale University Press 1989.

Gadamer, Hans Georg, *Truth and Method*. London 1975.

Gadamer, Hans Georg, *L'art de comprendre: Herméneutique et tradition philosophique. Ecrit 1 et* 2. Paris, Aubier 1991.

Gibbs, G., *Improving the Quality of Student Learning*. Bristol: Technical and Education Services, 1992 .

Gibson, Elaine & Levin, Harry, *The Psychology of Reading*. Cambridge, Mass., 1975.

Goldmann, Lucien, *Pour une sociologie du roman*. Paris 1965.

Gombrich, E.H., *Art and Illusion*. Princeton University Press 1960.

Good, Thomas L. &. Brophy, Jere E., *Educational Psychology: A Realistic Approach*. New York, Longman 1990.

Green, Diana, *What is Quality in Higher Education?* Society for Research into Higher Education & Open University Press 1995.

Greimas, A-J., *Du sens. Essais sémiotiques*. Paris 1970.
Halliday, M.A.K., *Learning how to Mean*. London 1975.
Halliday, M.A.K., *Language as Social Semiotic*. London 1978.
Hirsch, Jr. E.D., *Validity in Interpretation*. Yale University Press 1967.
Hirsch, Jr. E.D., *The Aims of Interpretation*. University of Chicago Press 1976.
Holland, Norman, *The Dynamics of Literary Response*. Oxford University Press 1968, 1975.
Holland, Norman, *Poems in Persons: An Introduction to the Psychoanalysis of Literature*. New York 1973, 1975.
Holzman, Michael, Theory, Research, and Pedagogy. *National Council of Teachers of English*, vol. 42, no. 4, December 1980.
Ingarden, Roman, *Das Literarische Kunstwerk*. Halle 1931.
Ingarden, Roman, *The Literary Work of Art: An Investigation on the Borderline of Ontology, Logic, and the Theory of Literature*. Northwest University Press 1973.
Iser, Wolfgang, *The Implied Reader: Patterns of Communication in Prose Fiction from Bunyan to Beckett*. Johns Hopkins University Press 1974.
Iser, Wolfgang, *The Act of Reading: A Theory of Aesthetic Response*. Johns Hopkins University Press 1978.
Janik, Dieter, *Die Kommunikationsstruktur des Erzählens: ein semiologisches Modell*. Rebenhausen: Rotsch 1973.
Jaspers, K., *The Idea of the University*. London: Peter Owen 1960.
Kayser, Wolfgang, *Das sprachliche Kunstwerk*. Bern 1959.
Knowles, M., *The Adult Learner: A Neglected Species*. Houston: Gulf Publishing Company 1978.
Koch, Kenneth, *Rose, Where Did You Get That Red? Teaching Great Poetry to Children*. New York: Vintage 1973.
Krieger, Murray & Dambo, Larry S., *Directions for Criticism: Structuralism and its Alternatives*. University of Wisconsin 1977.
Kuhn, T.S., *The Structure of Scientific Revolutions*. Chicago 1962.
Langer, Susanne K., *Philosophy in a New Key*. Cambridge, Mass., 1967.

Leavis, F.R., *The Living Principle*. London 1975.

Leavis, Q. D., *Fiction and the Reading Public*, 2nd ed., London 1968.

Leech, Geoffrey N., *A Linguistic Guide to English Poetry*. London 1969.

Lubbock, Percy, *The Craft of Fiction*. London 1961.

Lukàcs, Georg, *The Theory of the Novel*. London 1971.

Macleod, Flora & Golby, Michael, Theories of Learning and Pedagogy: Issues for Teacher Development. *Teacher Development*, vol. 7, no. 3, 2003.

McQuade, Donald A., *The Territory of Language: Linguistics, Stylistics, and the Teaching of Composition*. Carbondale, University of Illinois Press 1986.

Mailloux, Stephen, *Interpretive Conventions: The Reader in the Study of American Fiction*. Ithaca: Cornell University Press 1982.

Meyerhoff, Hans, *Time in Literature*. University of California Press 1955.

Neman, Beth S., *Teaching Students to Write*. 2nd ed. Oxford University Press 1995.

Newkirk, Thomas, *To Compose: Teaching Writing in the High School*. Portsmouth NH: Heinemann 1986.

Nias, J., and Groundwater-Smith, S. (eds.), *The Enquiring Teacher: Supporting and Sustaining Teacher Research*. London, Falmer Press 1988.

Nightingale, Peggy & O'Neill, Mike, *Achieving Quality Learning in Higher Education*. Kogan Page Limited, London 1997.

Nowottny, Winifred, *The Language Poets Use*. London 1965.

Ogden, C. K. & Richards I.A., *The Meaning of Meaning*. London 1923.

Olsen, Flemming, *Elements of Textual Analysis*. Copenhagen, Gyldendal 1986.

Olsen, Flemming & Søndergaard, Birgit, *Active Communication*. Copenhagen, Samfundslitteratur 2000.

Olsen, Flemming, *Between Positivism and T.S. Eliot: Imagism and T.E. Hulme*. University Press of Southern Denmark 2008.

Olsen, Flemming, *Eliot's 'Objective Correlative': Tradition or Individual Talent*. Sussex Academic Press 2012.
Olsen, Flemming, *The ut pictura poesis: Tradition and English Neo-Classical Landscape Poetry*. University Press of Southern Denmark 2013.
Peirce, Charles Sanders, *Chance, Love, and Logic: Philosophical Essays*. New York 1968.
Peters, R.S., *Education and the Development of Reason*. London: Routledge & Kegan Paul 1972.
Petterson, Torsten, 'Incompatible Interpretations of Literature'. *Journal of Aesthetics and Art Criticism*, vol. xlv, no. 2, Winter 1986.
Popperwell, Ronald G. (ed.), *Expression, Communication, and Experience in Literature and Language*. London, The Modern Humanities Research Association 1973.
Pratt, Mary Louise, *Towards a Speech Theory of Literary Discourse*. Indiana University Press 1977.
Propp, Vladimir, *Morphology of the Folktale*. American Folklore Society, Biographical & Special Series, vol. 9. Philadelphia 1958.
Quignard, Pascal, *Le lecteur*. Paris 1976.
Raban, Jonathan, *The Technique of Modern Fiction*. London 1968.
Radford, John, Raaheim, Kjell, de Vries, Peter & Williams, Ruth, Quantity and Quality in Higher Education. *Higher Education Policy Series*, 40. Jessica Kingsley Publishers, London & Bristol, Pennsylvania 1997.
Ray, William, *Literary Meaning*. Oxford 1984.
Reeves, James, *Understanding Poetry*. London 1965.
Reichert, John, *Making Sense of Literature*. University of Chicago Press 1977.
Richards, I.A., *Practical Criticism*. London 1929.
Richards, I.A., *How to Read a Page*. London 1967.
Ricoeur, Paul, *Le conflit des interprétations*. Paris 1969.
Ricoeur, Paul, *La métaphore vive*. Paris 1975.
Ricoeur, Paul, *Interpretation Theory: Discourse and the Surplus of Meaning*. Texas Christian University Press 1976.
Riffaterre, Michel, *Essais de stylistique structurale*. Paris 1971.

Riffaterre, Michel, *Production du texte*. Paris 1979.

Robin, Alexander, Still no Pedagogy? Principle, Pragmatism, and Compliance in Primary Education. *Cambridge Journal of Education*, vol. 34, no. 1, March 2004.

Rosenblatt, Louise, *Literature as Exploration*. New York 1937, 1968.

Rosenblatt, Louise, *The Reader, the Text, the Poem: The Transactional Theory of the Literary Work*. Southern Illinois University Press 1978.

Routh, Jane & Wolff, Janet (eds.), *The Sociology of Literature: Theoretical Approaches*. University of Keele 1977.

Schmidt, Barbara Herrnstein, *On the Margins of Discourse: The Relation of Literature to Language*. University of Chicago Press 1979.

Scholes, Robert & Kellogg, Robert, *The Nature of Narrative*. Oxford University Press 1966.

Scholes, Robert, *Fabulation and Metafiction*. University of Illinois Press 1979.

Searle, John R., *Speech Acts: An Essay in the Philosophy of Language*. Cambridge 1969.

Searle, John R. (ed.), *The Philosophy of Language*. Oxford Readings in Philosophy. London 1971.

Searle, John R., *Expression and Meaning: Studies in the Theory of Speech Acts*. Cambridge University Press 1981.

Segre, Cesare, *Semiotics and Literary Criticism*. The Hague: Mouton 1975.

Showalter, Elaine, *Teaching Literature*. Blackwell 2002.

Singleton, Charles S. (ed.), *Interpretation: Theory and Practice*. Johns Hopkins University Press 1969.

Slatoff, Walter, *With Respect to Readers: Dimensions of Literary Response*. Cornell University Press 1970.

Sontag, Susan, *Against Interpretation*. Farrer, Strauss & Giroux 1966.

Staiger, Emil, *Grundbegriffe der Poetik*. Zürich 1946.

Steiner, George, *On Difficulty*. Oxford University Press 1980.

Suleiman, Susan & Crosman, Inge (eds.), *The Reader in the Text: Essays on Audience and Interpretation*. Princeton University Press 1980.

Sunesen, Bent, *Towards a Theory of Foreign-Language Literature Teaching: Some Controversial Suggestions for Discussion among Teachers of English as a Central Subject in Danish Schools*. Copenhagen, Danmarks Lærerhøjskole 1975.

Sunesen, Bent, *In the Key of the Key: A Collection of Readings in the Theory and Practice of Literature Teaching, with Notes, Comments, Queries, Illustrative Material and Exercises for the Use of Teachers of English*. Copenhagen, Danmarks Lærerhøjskole 1977.

Taylor, G., Ballard, B., Bock, V., Chomsky, H.K., and Nightingale, P., *Literacy by Degrees*. Milton Keynes: SRHE and Open University Press 1988.

Todorov, Tzvetan, *Littérature et signification*. Paris 1967.

Todorov, Tzvetan, *Poétique de la prose*. Paris 1971.

Todorov, Tzvetan, *Symbolisme et interprétation*. Paris 1978.

Tompkins, Jane (ed.), *Reader Response Criticism*. Johns Hopkins University Press 1980.

Trilling, Lionel, *Beyond Culture*. New York 1967.

Waldmann, Günter, *Kommunikationsästetik I–II*. Munich 1975.

Walsh, William, *A Human Idiom*. London 1964.

Walvoord, Barbara Fassler, *Helping Students to Write Well: A Guide for Teachers in All Disciplines*. 2nd ed. New York: MLA 1982.

Watkins, Evan, *The Critical Act: Criticism and Community*. Yale University Press 1978.

Wellek, René & Warren, Austin, *Theory of Literature*. New York 1949.

Whorf, Benjamin Lee, *Language, Thought, and Reality*. Cambridge, Mass. 1956.

Wimsatt, W.K., *The Verbal Icon*. University of Kentucky Press 1954.

Young, R., *A Critical Theory of Education*. Hemel Hempstead, Harvester Wheatsheaf 1989.

Zimmermann, Bernhard, *Literaturrezeption im historischen Prozess: Zur Theorie einer Rezeptionsgeschichte der Litteratur*. Munich 1977.

Index

www.ingramcontent.com/pod-product-compliance
Lightning Source LLC
Chambersburg PA
CBHW070654100726
47907CB00007B/2207
9781845198251